Heartfelt Snippets
with
Moments of Magic

Martha Maggie Miller

Acknowledgements & Dedication

Heartfelt Snippets was the result of a lifetime of writing poetry only shared with close friends. In 2015 I compiled it into a manuscript in response to the urging of very special people, with the help of Vicki Arnett and Shirley Brantingham, and shared it with friends and family. Publishing a real book was not something I had ever considered. The fact that there are people who like what I have to say and want to read my work is still astounding to me. I have taken the content of *Heartfelt Snippets* and combined it with new work written since 2015 to create *Heartfelt Snippets with Moments of Magic.* The way I have put this book together does not comply with the rules and traditions that generally govern books of poetry. I acknowledge this, and provide that I have never been one who tended toward blind obedience. I hope you enjoy it.

This book is dedicated, first, to my husband, Steve, for putting up with my moments of escape into my own world, which happen frequently and leave him completely behind. Thank you for tolerating all of the times you have been speaking to me in one ear while my muse is whispering in the other and holding all of the space in between, which ultimately results in my asking, 'What did you say?' Next, to my parents, Richard and Donna Lee Strode, for encouraging my love of reading and creative writing when I was very young. Finally, to my Godparents, Tom and Donna M. Strode for encouragement, feedback in laughter and tears, and for championing my cause as I grew up when I couldn't do it myself. You are loved more than you could possibly know.

For everyone who has encouraged me to write, provided feedback, constructive criticism and bolstered my self-confidence, I say a big and heartfelt thank you. Without all of you, I would still be hiding my work and thinking it's not worth sharing. Each poem captures a piece of my soul and provides a conduit to my innermost thoughts. Sharing is the equivalent of laying my soul out for public comment and possible ridicule. This is very uncomfortable, and would have been impossible without the encouragement I have received. Thank you for showing interest. Thank you for pushing. Thank you for caring.

Additionally, a very special thank you to Vicki Arnett and Beverly Ulaszek for reviewing my work during the development of this book and providing honest and insightful comments. Your input guided the overall appearance and content of the finished product. You are both amazing women for whom I have the highest level of respect and a great deal of love.

Table of Contents

Service and Sacrifice

God Is Great and Mother Nature Rocks

Fur-Babies Make Us Better Humans

Music Ignites the Soul

Whimsy and Imagination

Life, Death and the Emotions Between

Mom

I feel you in the wind
Rain drops are your caress
I see you in the flowers and buzzing bees
I hear you in birds' song and windchimes
I smell you in the beauty of a rose

A Quiet Man

My father was a sinner.
My father was a saint.
My father was a good man
with rarely a complaint.

Just Breathe

The windchimes continue
to make joyful music on the mourning breeze.

The sun continues
to caress the landscape with its warming graze.

The minutes continue
to flow like a river from placid to cascade.

I continue to breathe.
I continue to grieve.

So this is what the world looks like
without you next to me.

Sorrow

He has come for a visit unexpectedly
and, like all unwanted guests,
has overstayed his welcome.
He hovers over your every activity,
a judgmental and demeaning intruder
finding fault, spewing criticism
with unsolicited advice and direction,
compounding your lethargy.
He ignores pointed suggestions
that he might find other accommodations
to be much more amusing
as he continues to feast
on your bounty and misery.
Until you reach the end of your tether,
gather your courage and strength,
and unceremoniously give him the boot.
Or succumb to his insidious influence
and drown as he watches…
dancing a jig at your final expense.

Communing with Dad (In a Tree Stand)

Dad…

The voice of nature surrounds me.
The breeze caresses my cheeks
and the cold bites exposed skin.
I feel you listening…
Your name becomes a whisper
sharing my innermost thoughts and fears
but most of all my overwhelming grief.
For a short time the pain eases…

*Written for my brother, Don Strode, whom
I love with my whole heart. Photos
provided by Don Strode.*

Forgiveness

She is a gentle woman
filled with love and empathy,
a soothing balm for your troubled soul,
your happiness her primary goal.
She purges festering sores and debrides burns,
stops hemorrhaging and cauterizes wounds.
She walks bravely through the briar of your emotions
protecting you from the backlash of flying monkeys.
She relieves you of your sensitivities
and clears the mine fields within your memories.
She facilitates your freedom to move forward,
lifts the weight and darkness you shoulder,
allows you to dance loose of burdens of the past
even though you may never fully understand.
She unravels the knots of your subconscious,
releases your heart from its barbed wire encapsulation.
She melts the steel of strife
giving you permission to let go of the fight.
Her greatest gift is acceptance and peace
a buoyancy of spirit and feeling of relief.

Entropy

A toothy smile
Blue eyes sparkling
Kind words on my lips
Direct eye contact
Easy laughter
Erect posture
Dressed professionally
Insightful responses to questions
Stillness without fidgeting
Photo frozen confidence

On my left the Lion is lagging
On my right trundles the Tinman
Toto is trotting jauntily nearby

Note: References to L. Frank Baum, "The Wizard of Oz"

Moments of Magic

Every time the muse inspires
a moment of clarity
enlightens the dark in spits and sparks,
a bubble of coalescing brilliance,
or a boiling witch's cauldron
wafting a crazy kaleidoscope
of swirling rainbow smog…

"Double, double toil and trouble;
Fire burn and caldron bubble."

Weaving words and imagery
with imagination into a sirens call,
rushing headlong into a maelstrom,
only to be hijacked by a tornado
tossed around by flying monkeys
and dropped unceremoniously
not on the original trajectory.

"Toto, I've a feeling
we're not in Kansas anymore…"

Moments of incandescent magic
captured in descriptive ink
ignite kinship infused with insight,
but divergent elucidation.
Filtered by personal experience
through a lens wreathed in reflection,
I witness others' thoughts take flight.

"To see a world in a grain of sand
And a heaven in a wild flower"

Note quotes from:
William Shakespeare, "Macbeth", "The Witches' Song"
L. Frank Baum, "The Wizard of Oz"
William Blake, "Auguries of Innocence"

Foundations

Always there to light the way.
Giving good advice even
when not accepted.
Never turning their backs
on your problems,
supporting even when they
feel you're wrong.
Loving you even when
you make mistakes.
Wanting your happiness
above their own.
Parents do all of
these things.
Providing you with a
solid foundation
from which to build
your whole life!

Family photo 1973

Daddy's Little Girl

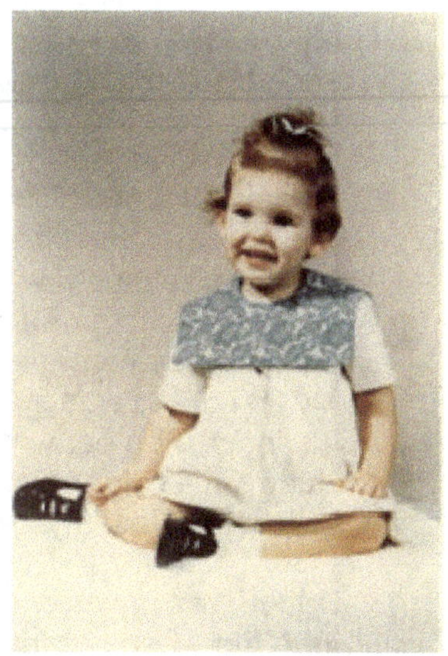

Me 1971

Daddy's little girl, that was me.
More comfortable climbing trees
than playing with effigies.
Fired my first gun with Daddy
supporting a rifle bigger than me.

My first biology lessons were experienced
hanging out in the garage when
Daddy returned a hunting success
with squirrels, quail, doves, rabbits and pheasants,
or in the back yard with a mess
of wiggling and flopping fish in the net,
bass, crappy, bluegill, mud cat and flat heads.

He would dress out the catch
under my watchful fascination,
naming the various parts and organs
defining function in his explanation,
peppered by a myriad of questions.

This is where I developed
my respect for the environment,
love for creatures scaled, furred and feathered,
saw my first glimpses of the food web,
realized human and animal dependence
on the natural resources endangered
by ignorance and enterprise.

My Daddy was a military man
and I followed his example
by joining the Army with a plan
for service and scholasticism
to make him proud of who I am.

I didn't date much, way too shy
clueless of the game and naïve,
too smart for most of the guys.
My first date I was so excited,
he showed up early in anticipation to find
Daddy, his Ruger and cleaning kit lying
in wait to divest my date of his juvenile desire.

Daddy was my eternal encouragement.
With me when I graduated…everything,
except the senior honors assembly
as I didn't anticipate the awards I accepted,
Daddy was upset he wasn't present.

He walked me down that beautiful aisle
when I found the man with whom I wanted to unite,
and I sang to him when we danced to Butterfly Kisses.

Always on the periphery of my years in the Army
right where I needed him to be.
Supporting dreams as I moved across the country
knowing I would be away from his security.

I called him Daddy when I was small
and regardless of how grown or mature,
Daddy he will be until I hear God's call.
No matter where life takes, me near or far,
Daddy's little girl I am deep in my heart.

Mama's Flower Garden

A place of beauty and peace
where busy minds can find sweet repose
relaxing in breezes filled with a myriad of scents
feeling warm sunlight filling you with contentment
while planting or admiring the variety of blooms
filling your soul deeply with joy and rejuvenation.

In Spring, warm sunlight and cool breezes
showcase the popping of daffodils and hyacinths,
the gentle advent of purple crocus,
red buds, dogwoods and lilacs;
tulips open with the colors of laughter;
bursting blooms of plunging peonies,
vibrant variants seen in the irises,
and the dancing of startled orange poppies.

Summer brings forth honeysuckle,
climbing clematis covers the archway of the gate,
crepe myrtle reaching for the sky in cones of glory,
roses seen in saturation and profusion.
The purple butterfly bush draws in the butterflies
enthroned in its little corner trying to rule indulgently.
Hibiscus and day lilies add their vivacious contribution.
Impatiens and geraniums are annually added with love
filling empty spaces and wooden flower pots.
Sunflowers voluntarily grow from Cardinal seed.
Birds flitting, bees bouncing from blossom to blossom.

Migration into Fall with a changing color pallet
to shades of red, gold and burgundy,
brilliant burning bushes from fuchsia to crimson
mums and marigolds flourishing in cooling breezes.
Flowers begin to wilt and fade, except the roses,
still throwing buds as the first frost feathers the ground
attempting to leach color only to magnify the spectacular
with a glazing of ice crystals that emblazon
brilliance and fragility as the sun strikes sparkles
sending them bouncing blindly into the sky.

Finally comes Winter and all fades to hushed secrecy,
awaiting the blanket of snow that inevitably falls,
dancing lightly through air like thistle in the breezes,
covering everything in wedding cake icing white.
There is beauty in icicles that drip drop from boughs
amplified in weak wintery light.
Diamonds glimmer like tiny blue flames in moonlight
with reflections of dazzling star bursts.
Renewal sleeps silently in replenishment
awaiting the warmth of sunlight and Mama's sweet call.

Mama's garden is a place of beauty and peace
where busy minds can find sweet repose
relaxing in breezes filled with a myriad of scents
feeling warm sunlight filling you with contentment
while planting or admiring the variety of blooms
filling your soul deeply with joy and rejuvenation.

The Picture of Health

There is a Polaroid I have I truly cherish
and selfishly refuse to share.
You are about one year old
dressed in the ugliest gold-colored onesy,
which absolutely had to be a gift
because I can't see Mom, even in her thrift,
buying for either of us to wear.
Your tow-headed white blond hair
is standing straight up
floating like downy duckling fluff.
You are running toward the camera
with both arms waving in the air
and the biggest brightest smile
on your face, whose glowing shine
could only be beaten by the light
sparkling in your pale blue eyes,
with apples in your cheeks reminiscent
of Santa in Coke commercials at Christmas.
You were leaning forward into your momentum
completely fearless and knowing your motion
would carry you straight into arms
that would never let you come to harm.
Obviously, you were a happy child
as laughter can still be heard echoing wildly
from the confines of this faded color photo
taken so many long years ago.
You were secure in the love that surrounded you
and radiant with the health of youth.
It's the only picture I have of you whole and unmarred
by events so shortly to occur.

My baby brother 1972

My Inspiration

My Brother and me, 1987

He defined the role of my youth…big sister;
responsibility, caretaker, foreman, defender,
companions from birth.
Who could resist those eyes and crooked little grin?
He was a pest, following me everywhere,
we fought like the Road Runner and Wile E Coyote.
Oh, the trouble we created…
a shattered mirror and a fractured finger
a broken door glass, a nail through a bare foot.
We were good at drying tears and cleaning up
but these we couldn't fix or hide.
He was mine to pick on and to protect;
those who caused him harm felt
the ferocity of a lioness with a cub.
He became my confidant
my co-conspirator
my best friend.
If he wasn't welcome,
there were better things to do,
accepted if my friends wanted me around.
He effortlessly overcame challenges that astounded
and became my inspiration.
I found myself looking up to him,
figuratively as well as literally.
Then I left for university…
three o'clock every day my phone would ring,
we'd talk until Mom's car pulled in
then hurriedly disconnect, never realizing
Mom paid the phone bill and never uttered a rebuke,
we missed each other fiercely and she knew.
As life has moved the chess board pieces
so much time and space has come between us
but not a day goes by
for my little brother and I
that we do not rely on the bond that exists
and continues each day to strengthen.
It's always been us against the world
my little brother and his big sister, Murph!!

A Snow Day

Giggles were rampant
snow had been falling for days.
Daddy was trying to clear a path
shoveling, scooping, pausing to aim
or duck snowballs flying at him.
The icy pile's nearest face
growing ever higher and bigger
as the shovels efforts are displaced.
Two little Eskimos all bundled
tunneling and creating a snow fort,
using it as an obstacle,
secure, if a bit short,
to launch missiles
at Daddy's turned back!!
Smack…smack…giggle…giggle,
he returned fire…Duck!!
Hysterical laughter echoed.
By the time Daddy's chore was finished
the two Eskimos had hollowed
and reinforced their fortress
inside the snow mountain
to withstand Daddy's onslaught,
at least, until he charged the fortification
and the Eskimos were caught.
Mama yelled out the appraisal
that we'd been outside long enough.
A fire was glowing,
hot chocolate already in mugs
with little marshmallows afloat
hotdogs laid out on long forks
and s'mores ready to roast
awaiting the refugees of the snow wars.
We knocked off the snowpack
dropped boots at the back door
hung wet snowsuits on the coat rack
with chatter overflowing
describing what transpired
arguing about who prevailed,
whose snowballs were biggest,
and who had the best aim,
Daddy or the Eskimos.

Time

A screaming cry starts the journey.
At first kicking as new muscles generate
then on the wobbly feet of a toddler
achingly slow as 12 1/2 waits impatiently for 13
like the rhythmic steps of a cross country runner
picking up speed with the kiss of every first.

Tic, tic, tic

The fluidity finds its intangible velocity.
Forcefully forward like a raging river
racing Mother Nature toward a waterfall,
sedately enjoying a campfire's comforting flicker
with hot chocolate and marshmallows burning,
rose petals' minuscule movement as they unfurl
through the dew to greet the warmth of morning,
or carving the landscape with the flow of a glacier.
Then there are moments when it seems to stop entirely
holding at forever on the point of a needle.

Tic, tic, tic

A thief siphoning means and vitality.
Overlooked for the challenge of the opportunity,
driven unaware from day to night, hour to minute,
paths through the forest converging inflexibly,
passage captured in moments of clarity
with reflection mirrored not on the mind's eye
denied by the finite beating of a heart blinded
even when evidence is hiding in plain sight;
in their music, language, self-righteousness, morality
and overwhelming sense of invulnerability.

Tic, tic, tic

The ever shrinking circle of influence.
Where there once was laughter and companionship
now exists a box of pictures faded and tattered
and memories trickling through antiquated technology
like a phone booth, floppy disc or telegraph,
left behind in the speed of light and electrons.

Tic, tic, tic

Petals of Life

Like the petals of a rose as it withers,
petals of your life are left everywhere you've been,
bread crumbs that define your trail.
What happens to them?
Do they leave a lasting impression,
or do they drift away like scent on the breeze?

If they are watered and cared for
maybe they take root to grow and flower.
Then the path through the garden,
sometimes straight, sometimes meandering,
but always flowing forward, rarely turning,
is marked by new growth unnoticed and unrealized.

In dark days of doubt
retracing your trail to previously unknown flowers
enlightens the way which wanders through the garden,
highlighting the unrealized impact of the petals of your life
on those touched and left behind.

Time of the Flower

The passing of one's time is as fleeting as that of the flower,
depending on one's view, from the seed or the bower.
The seed struggles continuously to break through the soil
in search of sunlight, insects and air; ever in toil.
It reaches the pinnacle of existence with the beauty of its bloom,
and is allowed to pause only shortly before fading to its doom.

A point will be reached in the passing of the seasons
where one will stop looking for reasons
to push time quickly, ever forward,
and will yearn greatly toward
that time when life was bright and sparkling new.
Be certain to live every second so no regrets spoil the view.

Waves to Ripples

Sometimes grief hits like high tide
with the violence of the swell
crashing against a cliff side
rolling over you in gut wrenching,
body racking, uncontrollable emotion
stealing your ability to breathe
severing muscle control
taking you out at the knees
tumbling you into the undertow
without the will to struggle free
so you drown in your sorrow.

Other times it flows in gently
like the surf at low tide
gliding over the sand rhythmically
silent tears falling steadily
welling up to overflow
washing your heart clean
soothing your troubled soul
allowing recovery's inevitable entry
abrading the open lesion
until an ugly scab develops
and your misery eases.

Finally, grief ripples across moments
like the wind over tidal pools, bereft,
in rocky crags or sandy depressions
left by the sea's recession.
Circles form concentrically
isolated and transient
tiny salt water biospheres
with echoes of beauty
glimmering through the tears
because happy memories
begin to overshadow the despair.

Insomnia

Oh sleep… thou elusive butterfly,
Benadryl will stretch forth its silken net
to capture thine ethereal beauty
and confine thee in its gilded cage.
Much to mine dismay
thine captivity is too ephemeral,
disrupted by illusive imagery
and perpetual nightmare.

Satori

Looking out through
the darkness of night
my imagination,
both vivid and wild,
sees a Tiger in majesty
burning bright
in the deepest forest,
so very frightening.
The shadows flicker
in sinuous motion
as the flames
continue to grow.
Drums in the distance,
in rhythm with the glow,
inflame my heart in epiphany,
I am not alone,
and my soul shatters
into a myriad of emotions.

Note: A reference to William Blake, "The Tyger"

Symbiosis

I am the music
that calms the soul
of the wild beast,
curbs the darkness,
tempers anger,
appeases distrust
and facilitates tact.

In exchange
you are my strength,
my security, my courage,
my confidence,
and the sealant
binding my fractures.

I bring the humor
that lights the sparkle
in your blue eyes,
inspiring amusement,
and belly deep laughter.
I illuminate
your softer side.

You are my lodestone,
holding true north,
my Basanite
whose mark reveals
real from fool's gold,
ever encouraging me
to chase my dreams.

You are strong
when I am weak.
You are sure
when I falter.
You question

while I have faith.
You see clearly
when I am oblivious.

We may not always
understand,
but we endeavor,
together, to love.

Building Blocks

I truly miss childhood memories we never made.
Those many times I would have been left behind
as my brothers went off on their bikes to fish,
to play sports or just hang out sharing confidences.
Those times my big brother would say "Come on, let's go"
just me and him for an hour or so
on an errand that was to me an adventure
riding around with the music blasting
on his awesome motorcycle
or with the windows open on his roadster,
feeling cool as my friends watched enviously,
feeling special and basking in his attention.
I missed growing up as the middle child.
Miles I'd have gotten out of my pouty lip and smile
he wouldn't have been able to resist my every whim,
and the mediator I would have been....
The little sister with a big brother she idolized
to follow around with little puppy eyes
to plague with her presence and childish inquisivity
to use as a threat to keep away all the bullies
to protect her from the big bad wolf
to set her path with teachers through school
to frighten perspective suitors to their best behavior
to show her the way to grow strong and true
to teach her that respect is earned and not given freely
providing an example of what a good person should be.
I wasn't there when you turned eighteen
to proudly say goodbye as you left to become a Marine.
No childhood memories do we share
but happy I am that I dared
to openly recognize my big brother
to open my heart to the love you offered.
Time we have to make up for missed memories
by not wasting a single opportunity
to share all of life's quirks and anomalies
cherishing each other as family
building a relationship based in friendship
mutual trust, love and respect.

Apple Pie

This sweet pervasive scent
conjures up a sweeter memory,
not of baseball or the American dream,
but of a pre-adolescent me...
Mama was on a mission to the store
and Daddy got to be chauffer.
Before they left I was promised
flaky gooey apple cinnamony deliciousness
of my most favorite dessert
if apples were peeled on their return!!
Trusted to be left alone with my brother
after repetition of grandparents' numbers
they left me standing on a chair at the sink
with a bowl full of apples just a paring.
The knife slipped
I screamed and jumped
blood started to flow.
Little brother became overwrought
as the blood would not stop
so two frantic phone calls made
my Grandpas arrived on the double.
Mama and Daddy came charging in,
prepared with remonstrations for shenanigans
due to the pink wrecker and red truck parked in front,
to see me at the kitchen table being comforted
with a Grandpa on the left and a Grandpa on the
my thumb swaddled in bandages held high
crying because the apples weren't done
and I felt the swoop of impending trouble.
Mama went from anger to laughter
before she could start her tirade
as she heard simultaneously uttered
"It's okay Moe" and "Now Donna"
as my Grandpas explained
the events that led to their presence.
My brother was rewarded for having good sense
and Mama quickly finished the task I was set
so the pie could be rushed into the oven
and served before my Grandpas departed
sedately returning home
with smiles and more to relay.

Fishing Frenzy

Perched precariously straddling the dam into Crane Lake
a swiftly trickling flow across the opening below
poles rigged out with corks and hooks baited
sun glistening off sweat and oil-slicked skin already
bronzed to toasted coconut from our summer escapades.
Parents in a flat bottomed, baby blue boat bobbing
in the slow, moving water of the Snicarte Slough
bow resting lightly on the sandy east bank
left exposed high and dry by the low water of August.
Ensuring Mom and us kids were baited and situated
Dad always, always, dropped his lines last.
Mom stretched leisurely in her lounge chair
sunshades gracing her face, floppy hat over blond hair,
with beer and book in hand awaiting first bite.
My little brother, who had forgone bass fishing
in fear of being out fished by his big sis,
had given up Shimano, rod, and flashing spinnerbait
to toss a cork on a dead line in the sunshine.
A flick of the wrist sent line floating through the air
a slight jolt and the worm dropped with a plop
the bright orange bobber dragged under popped up
then sat idly buoyant for a millisecond
before sinking again in the aggressive, greedy
jaws of a hungry willow catfish. The toothless pest
and I had found a fishy feeding frenzy.
One after the other alternating from little brother to me
up and over the dam, into Dad's unexpecting lap to unhook
and back into the water went the bait and bobber.

No time in between for Dad to deploy his own lines.
Giggles regaled as we bounced and danced
joyously indulging our glee at Dad's obvious irritation.
His grumbles and growls join the chorus
sprinkled with the chainmail-like tinkling of the livesack,
the splashing and wriggling of flipping fins and tails,
as it was raised, filled and dropped with our catch.
Mom's admonishments not to fall in
sporadically interrupted by her unsuccessful attempts
to hide her own laughter joined the refrain.
To his complete and utter dismay
Dad never did get to actually fish that day.
and my life was enriched with a memory to share
which glows as brightly in my mind's eye
as the sun, joy and musical laughter that echoes
in the retelling still this many years later.

Joy

She is an aloof and evasive butterfly.
Full of color and graceful motion
whispering wings waving and fluttering
dancing just beyond your nose,
an image of what you cannot attain.
She darts in to gently kiss your cheek,
but before you can wrap her in an embrace
she gracefully rises out of reach,
grazes you with a sympathetic gaze
and teasingly floats away on the breeze.

Crushed

Each time I closed my eyes relaxing into sleep
I could feel the heavy shadows undefined
of an infinite monolith perched precariously over me.

Silently it would fall and I would jerk awake.
As it was about to crush me with its weight
I would sit up straight my teeth rattling in terror.

The first time this illusory image was felt
Mama's comforting arms were withheld.
She thought I just sought attention.

So Daddy tucked me in, kissed my ear
and told me he'd be near,
there was nothing to fear.

The glow and low volume of the television
lulled me into false somnolence
and I slipped into sleepy lethargy.

The heavy shadows would blanket me
over and again I would wake screaming
as Daddy's patience grew lean.

Exhaustion finally won
in the wee hours before dawn
and we slept totally wrung.

With morning light bright and sunny
Daddy warned me angrily
this was a first and last exigency.

Subsequently when slumber was interrupted
I would sneak to the foot of my parent's bed
and comfort myself with their presence.

Mama would trip over me in the morning
astonished I was asleep on the floor
and tease me about not being a big girl.

Purgatory

Darkness fills my chest and squeezes my heart
as the movie projector of my mind starts
its universally identifiable clickity clickity clicking
and the film begins to roll, lighting up the screen.

Time slows to a crawl as the unknown pattern
opens before me in the warp and weft of the fabric
trapping me in its weave, ever constricting,
in an infinitesimally slow, disjointedly repeated riff.

My movements become microns
as my nervous system fails to fire;
my brain recognizes the impending threat
but my eyes see no path to circumvention
and my tongue swells in my mouth
leaving no room for words or breath.

Her demeanor is menacing as she scrutinizes
a chore to be done before homework, incomplete,
my movements slow, methodical and silent
with stubbornness and infinitesimal defiance.
Like an Egyptian task master over an obstinate slave,
she retaliates with a back hand to the face.

Pain seers my cheek laterally
blossoming with the ringing in my ear
as my pearl stud earring flies free
and the floor becomes reacquainted with my knees.

I didn't quickly regain my feet and return to task
so she yanks upward on my ponytail until I'm standing
like the Scarecrow's introduction to Dorothy.
Her diatribe continues to castigate me
while I shift clothes from washer to dryer
listening to her call me names and mock my misery
threatening more excessive brutality
because I was moving too slowly.

The film springs free of the reel
adding a periodic slap to the clickety clicking.
A flaw in the textile trap opens a gaping hole
easing the tension and releasing my soul
like steam from a teapot on the stove hissing
I realize 35 years later that pearl earring is still missing.

Matriarch

The photo does her no justice.
Black and white does not disclose evidence
of eyes as bright as the clearest sky.
It's from a time that hides
the sparkle in their eyes and true nature.
It fails to share the narrative
of a heart endlessly full of love,
laughter, joy and hope…
kindness, empathy, forgiveness and wisdom;
the complete depiction of a Christian woman.

Of light and goodness she was the epitome,
an example to hold aloft of what we should aspire to be.

The photo does no justice to
her dedication to family through
times of plenty and dearth;
times of pain and mirth,
with dignity and perseverance.
She was strong by design, not by chance,
with a heart of gold and strong convictions.
From her, nothing could be hidden,
once caught in her gaze all was quickly revealed
and your fate sealed!

Her family was not defined by blood alone,
but encompassed all who entered her home.

The photo does not adequately depict
the strength of her character.
She was the salve to heal all wounds
and, holding all together, the glue.
She was quick to defend and shield,
and always the voice of reason.

Ethel Irene Strode

Dorothy Ann Tuxhorn

The teacher, the baker, the candlestick maker,
the nurse, the seamstress, the story teller,
the disciplinarian, the cheering squad,
the spoiler and the confidant.

She was everything to some and special to most.
The photo isn't perfect, but she was very close.

What Did I Say?

Heartfelt and fleeting
words spoken through great emotion

Feelings elicited branded on memory
    lessening of pain
        laughter through tears

And on the opposite horizon
    excitation of rage
        deepening of despair

But the words remain forever lost
locked in the moment of expression

A Single Tear

How can something so unpretentious
have so many different interpretations
as a single solitary tear?
Sorrow and love, anger and fear,
laughter and jubilation.
A small drop of saline
leaking from the soul's mirror
to leave a glistening indication
of pervasive emotion overflowing,
made more significant by its singularity
and the absolute unfamiliarity.
That a tear would have the temerity
of traversing this beloved visage
is both wondrous and incredible.
Joyfully branded on my memory
a sign of such immensity
in the breadth of love and emotion
my grandfather felt for me.
An image I will take to the grave
on my mind's eye forever engraved
of arms outstretched and waiting
to sweep me into a bearish embrace.
Looking into that so loved face
and knowing the single tear that traced
its slow and agonizing escape
was for me alone, my tears kept pace.
This was the one and only time
I ever saw my grandfather cry
this impression of his love and pride
will be with me until the day I die.
I hear his voice periodically in my head
even though the words were never said
I know he loved me definitively
because of the single tear he shed.

John F. Tuxhorn, Jr.

Homesick

Heard from my college dorm room
on a cool spring night with windows
wide for sweet breezes wafting floral,
distant achingly haunting music
of a train's whistle floating away,
approaching a rural railway crossing
warning bells chime adding harmony.
The oh-so-lonely melody brings to mind
a rumbling carried more clearly on stillness…
The sound of the engine winding up
gradual movement of a car
crash of one slamming into another
thunk as the coupling system locks into place
followed by the smaller jolting and banging
as they move into synchronicity
echoing repeatedly until all are tamed to the lead.
The engine grinds and groans again
I… think… I… can… I. Think. I. Can. I think I can…
as it pulls the cars down the tracks,
like a kid dragging his security blankey,
picking up speed as it heads
toward darkness and freedom.
I return from my psychogenic moonlit trip
gaze around my snug tumultuous escape
seeing all the signposts of my liberation
then turn and pick up the phone
reaching for family and home.

Twice Blessed....

Blessed am I with my first Dad
a role model and little girl's hero
loving my Mom through good and bad
arriving in the nick of time the day I was born
who raised me with love and respect to form
the person I have become.

A military man, he gave me discipline,
taught me the importance of honesty and laughter
A soft-hearted man he taught me compassion
and through his love of nature, set me on my life's path.

Twice blessed am I
to have received my second Dad
the day I wed my lifemate
and was accepted with open arms into his family,
one of the kindest and most caring of souls
with a big heart to match his joyful glow.

My beloved's Dad by choice – not by blood,
sharing his love of motorcycles and philosophy on life
he raised a boy not his own with a Father's love
and took me as a daughter when I became his son's wife.

Twice by God have I been blessed,
to be loved by two such wonderful men.

Wedding photos: me and Dad, and our
Best Man, Jack Miller, my father-in-law

My Shelter from the Storm

I awaken in your arms in the night
feeling safe, secure and warm,
even as the storm tortures the dark
and leaves the landscape torn.
Lightning flashes an eerie daylight as I
snuggle into your masculine form.
Your arms settle me closer still and
a contented sigh to me is borne
on the breath that penetrated our window
to escape the fervor of the storm.
You are my shelter from terrors
borne by black shadow's courtship.
Through the nightmares
and the thrashing,
my only fluorescence.
The strength of your arms even in sleep
insulates me against all horror
surrounds me with your love
and I rest oblivious to the turmoil.

The Human Plight

Evil makes a home in the heart of every soul...
The truly virtuous fight a constant battle
with their dark companion for control
waging war on the seven deadly sins and rattling
courageously the shield of conscience
drawing the line with morality, love and kindness.

The Gift

It was a beautifully wrapped box
that neither rattled or knocked,
a bauble for a child to admire.
I never thought to inquire
nor the contents to discern
until a star fell away from my journey.
The tag was engraved
with a progression of names.
Names of people dear
among which mine appeared.
I wonder why I have never looked inside,
what could the wrapping be hiding?
It at first appeared empty ---
but it whispered to me
look closer, look deeper…
Courage was buried in the tissue paper,
Pride and Strength were there also.
Suddenly the box was overflowing!!
Faith, Love, Forgiveness, Honesty…
Creativity, Intelligence, Hope, and Curiosity…
Each floated as a brilliant light
straight to my heart.
True realization enveloped me
and warmth enfolded eternally.
This gift had been passed from parents to children
generation to generation
wrapped beautifully in concealment
until wisdom and enlightenment emerge.

The tag was engraved
with a progression of names.
As I watched, a name began to glow… and then to fade.

Dinner with Grandpa

Last night as I lay sleeping
I had dinner with my Grandpa.
It was just him and me
in the kitchen at Mama's.
His apparition was hale and hearty
as he was when I was young,
with smile, glasses and unlit cigar.
We spoke of things major and mundane
including my life's choices,
a dialog of encouragement and faith.
We ate pasta with red sauce
heated on a futuristic hot plate
filling the air with delicious aroma.
Companionably across the counter
we shared messy slurpy fun
as scent became sound and laughter.
A vase was there on the table
holding a bouquet of posies
to which I supplemented
crystalline strands of memory
projected movie-style on the wall.
Grandpa grabbed a broom
and, dancing, kept me enthralled
tapping out a rhythm on hardwood
tap… tap, tap, tap, swoosh…
tap…tap, tap, tap…swish…
elusive as I tried to swipe the corn.
Your Mom used to sweep this way
making music as she worked
adding pleasure to the day.
I awoke startled from my dream
bubbling with joy and laughter
refreshed and at ease
secure in the warmth of his love.

Just Stopping By

I awaken from the sweetest dream
filled with anticipation and wellbeing.
I stopped by to find the door locked
but my hand knowingly finds the key,
where it's always been in a hidden little box.
I open the box to find a key, a $10 bill, and a note
written in the beloved hand of a beautiful lady:
"I'm not here," it says, "but make yourself at home,"
the letters legibly composed but shaky.
It goes on to say, "Stay as long as you need.
If you're hungry, the 'fridge holds plenty,
if thirsty there is always fresh iced tea,
if you're sleepy, the couch is comfy.
If there is something you want not already here
use the money tucked in with the key.
Pop on down to the store nearby,
grab what you need and an extra for me.
I promise I'll be back shortly."
Tears swell and drip from my chin
as reality replaces the dream
filling me with an unpleasant image.
Nothing of Grandma's house is left
after the bulldozer was unchained.
All that remains is a grassy prominence
surrounded by sidewalk and driveway.
Never again, just on a whim, can I stop on the fly
for a hug and a sweet smile simply to say Hi.

Friendship

Sunshine on a Spring day.
Secrets and struggles shared.
Earth after a down pour.
Salt elevating life's flavor.
Fresh cut grass and lilacs in bloom.
A freshly painted room.
The first breath of a newborn.
Hushed quiet of an Easter morn.
Puppy breath and kittens purring.
Unbridled tear-streaming laughter.
Crickets and frogs and lightning bugs.
A bone cracking bear hug.
Wind whipped hair on a joy ride.
Feet in the sand at high tide.
Water's trickling music tickling fingers.
Answering a ring at two in the morning.
A shoulder when heartbroken.
Snug by a fire watching snowflakes float.
Rhythmically blinking Christmas lights.
Big issue discussions without a fight.
Understanding another's truth.
Freedom to just be you.

Laura

The other half of my soul
is the sister of my heart
and my best friend.

Nurturing to my ego
light to my dark
water to my flame.

She balances me
and makes me complete.

Separated by miles
but never by distance
closer today than yesterday.

Sharing tears and smiles
no judgment or resistance
ever lighting my way.

The other half of my soul
the one who makes me whole
the sister of my heart
is my best friend.

Elizabeth

Strength has a name,
she is called Elizabeth.
She faces Adversity daily,
meets him face-to-face
with calm and self-assurance,
and beats him on his own turf.
She is the master of Pain
holding him lassoed and hog-tied.
She calls Positivity and
Determination friends,
and, with Hope, she perseveres.
Her friends support her fully
through every leg of her journey,
taking all of life's obstacles
like an Olympic relay runner
intent on a Gold Medal.
She is true to her beliefs
and steadfast in her convictions.
Strength, her name is Elizabeth.

Family snapshot, 1988

The Fog of Grief

Just for a moment
as I lay in bed,
floating peacefully
between awake and asleep,
I saw your smiling images
and for an instant
forgot you're deceased.
I thought of something
I wanted to share with you.
The idea moved
like a warm hug
across my subconscious
that I'd call in the morning.
We'd share a bit of humor,
have a nice conversation.
Then reality rushed in,
with a touch of incredulity,
on a wave of grief
and drowsiness fled
for more than a moment.

Serendipity

There are those who are transient,
Fleeting...
And those who are eternal,
Immutable....
Impact is not influenced solely by longevity
but by sharing tears and tales.

Genesis

He has his momma's eyes
and his Grandpa's smile.
Look at those dimples.
We haven't seen those since
Great Uncle Jim.

Doting parents and grandparents
staking claim in shared attributes.

She has her Grandma's nose
and her Grandpa's crooked toes.
Look at that curly dark hair!!
We haven't seen that since
Great Aunt Clair.

Pictorial evidence unearthed
of similarities defined before birth.

Hands aging to look like Grandma's,
blonde hair darkened with a reddish cast.
Historic characteristics echoing ancestors,
startling epiphanies.

Changes continue to slowly emerge
influenced by nature and nurture.

Photos taken by Amanda Camden Photography

Traces

Traces of kindness
an unanticipated helping hand

Traces of confidence
a grin and jaunty step

Traces of happiness
echoing laughter

Traces of maturity
respectful demeanor

Traces of wisdom
kind words softly spoken

Traces of partnership
intimacy in a gentle touch

Traces of worry
silver streaked hair

Traces of time
a weathered and lined face

Traces of the race
sharp aches and pains

Traces of great loss
sorrow deep in the eyes

Traces of God
a humble and loving heart

Traces of love
innumerable.

Fragmentation

Chicken Little is without his refrain
the world has not been immolated
the sun still dances across her stage
but my world continues sideways.
Like a square wheel on a steep hill
my rock has melted into quicksand
my foundation sundered by quake
echoes of mocking phrases reverberate
surround sound in stereo reprise.

Personification

Giving faces to your emotions.
Assigning human characteristics
so realistically enervated
that they start talking to you,
judging your thoughts,
questioning your decisions,
undermining your motivation.
Action and inaction…

Ode to the Fisherman

The sky is a beautiful clear blue
the sun is shining brightly
the wind is a gently blowing breeze
and the bugs joyfully buzzing.

The fisherman gets the itch.

It could be overcast, clouds all dingy
with the sun playing hide 'n' seek
between rain drops soaking the seat
on the boat rocking and creaking.

And the fisherman STILL gets the itch,

to hear the quiet sounds of nature
feel the wriggling of the bait.
Whir goes the line, plop the weight
and the circular ripples spread and abate.

Ahhhh, tranquility the fisherman sighs.

In quiet solitude the fisherman waits
watching the rod for any slight shake
to see the fish take the bait
the hook set, rod jerked, reeling in no haste.

Triumph! The fisherman grins!

The live sack is hung off the side of the boat
tied securely as it bounces and floats
with the movement of fishy fins, swirls noted
awaiting the next addition to be loaded.

The fisherman has only one regret.
His favorite companions are otherwise engaged
and couldn't go fishing this day
his granddaughters are growing up so far away
he missed their joyful voices and happy play.

He calls to tell them how much he cares,
misses their company and to gloat a comparison
of where he is without them there,
simply to share.

The fisherman falls not wearing a life vest.

On this beautiful day with the bugs a buzzing
the water sends ripples out in slow circling
where the fisherman's boat is found floating
his hat retrieved by searchers wet and soaking.

The fisherman met God doing what he loved best.

Photo provided by Alicia Strode

Depression

The fog closes in around me,
engulfing but nebulous,
with movement and moments of clarity,
a thick and isolating opaque
monochromatic grayscale airily
ranging from bright to dark.
The Sun struts in to illuminate
and disperse the oppression,
arrogantly casual in her certitude
that burning success will follow.
Teased by Hope as glimmers
of light melt the mist,
I can see enough to identify
those who are absent
and the mountain that needs my attention.
Apathy steps in, pulls the curtain
and the gloom seeps anew,
deeper, darker and more pervasive.
The Sun contritely concedes
to the pull of the Moon.
He whispers softly in my dreams
taking a gentler, more subtle approach,
bringing the stars along as company
to remind me of happier times,
to dispel the fog with love and security,
in an attempt to empower Hope,
providing true north for safe navigation.
But Hope is crushed once more
under shadows insidiously slinking,
grabbing at my hair, tearing at my face,
raking claws over my skin
like being caught in a briar
or lost in a corn field without direction.
Panicking, screaming my throat bloody,
blindly racing toward whispers
heard in the mist, I smack into a door...

for which I have no key... nose first,
bounce and slide bonelessly to the floor,
spent and exhausted.
Outside the door, laughter implores
beckoning with invitation.
Hope's presence in the mist
becomes a wavering and fading mirage,
Yearning is smothered by a pillow
as the opacity of the fog returns,
more comforting in comparison,
while Stasis gathers my tears.

Euphoria

After days and nights of overwhelming
continuous and excruciating pain
She washes slowly over you
coating you like warm honey,
enveloping you in warm and fuzzy,
from the top of your head
to the tips of your toe nails.
For those few moments
your heart beats full and languorous,
every inch of your skin tingles,
every breath you take is sweet,
and you float on a smile,
as she soothes away your pain.

Fifty

I scrutinize my surroundings,
turning slowly in a circle.
Where once life was blue skies
and wildflower filled fields
buzzing with opportunities and choices
I have now reached the lookout
on the summit of a mountain.
A precipice from which there is
only one way... down,
but not the same way I got here...
that way is an impediment
of seemingly impossible obstacles.
How I got to this pinnacle in the clouds
is foremost in my mind
as I review my limited options
for forward momentum or regression.
And where is the sky ride that services
this ski slope?
The most obvious route
to sea level appears treacherous,
makes my knees hurt just viewing,
is steep with loose chert and flaking rock,
boulders and huge trees blocking the path,
crevices that turn into canyons,
and is that quicksand??
Really??
I'm paralyzed by confusion
as I work to discern my predicament...
I thought time was my friend
and would always have my back,
when, in fact, it was the wave
under my surfboard swiftly lifting
and throwing me toward a distant shore.
In the flutter of an eyelash,
the twinkle of that distant wishing star,
half my life is behind me
and the nefarious bus driver

who dumped me on this spot,
which by the by was nowhere
in my travel itinerary,
without a compass, a map, a touchstone,
stars inconveniently hidden by clouds
through which the moon plays peekaboo,
to guide me or give directional orientation.
I am lost in a vortex without goals,
fat lot of good strategic planning did me...
Always have a Plan B,
be flexible to roll with the punches
and deal with the fruit life throws,
whether fresh or rotten.
I shout as loudly as the limited air
on the mountain will allow -
DO OVER!! I want a do over!!
That is not the card I wanted to play!!
Especially now that I see
it was the move that lost me the game.
Hindsight is a tortuous bitch.
I am really not ready to tumble
the downward trek...
So I do what Clara did when she
followed The Doctor into the park.
Doctor Who?... you might ask...
I start searching the air above my head
jumping for the bottom rung
of that invisible ladder
which will take me to the blue box.

Photo taken by Steve Miller

Alzheimer's, the Dissolution of Self

Self is the whole of its memories,
big moments and small,
formative experiences,
some temporarily lost to time,
but resurrected by scent, sound or sight
as déjà vu crystallizes in realization.

Memories dissolved by disease
float away into mist
and what of Self is left?
Frustration in actions started,
stopped short in confusion.
Crushing fear in free fall
with anticipation of agony
vented on loved ones,
helpless to cease.
Anger and frustration
ride the tide of fear,
hopelessness consorts with grief.

A life's essence, imbued
with past and present,
is cradled in memory.
How can Self yet identify

ideals of greatest import,
beliefs, values, and love,
and recognize their reflection?

Kin previously deceased,
remembered for molding
psyche and persona,
become victims of true death
perpetuated by loss of Self.
Forever gone, the last avenue
of existence destroyed.

Angels' wings flash lucidity.
Hope and faith fashion
the double-edged sword
wielded by God's grace
illuminating episodic clarity.
Gratitude fights nausea and pain
watching memory dissolve
and slide the slippery slope.

Does God gather memories,
unfettered and astray....
safeguard them with loving care
blessedly restored in His presence?

Migraine

Moving through my daily routine initially
with a smile for everyone and high energy
gradually slowing becoming quiet and grumpy
withdrawn, irritable and sensitive.

My sparkle becomes oxidized copper
a nasty chest deep grumble colors my speech
painting my perception of all encounters
in tarnished blacks and greens.

My eyes are narrowed and twitching
my attempts at forming sentences feeble
working through a fog for cohesiveness
the glue holding my words vanishing.

My hair has committed some grievance
for which pulling and tugging is the penalty
as my hands move unconsciously
to carry out this involuntary judgment.

Wan and pale of visage
the vice at the base of my skull tightens
as the building pressure begins
and my shoulder muscles spasm for attention.

Everything is so glaring and vociferous
my stomach starts to heave and gurgle
the application of the ice pick is initiated
and my world is reduced to a garish red.

Red seen through the thinness of my closed eyes
curled in the darkness like a fetus
trying to shut out the world entirely
while the pain with my heart stabs and beats.

Tossing and turning impotently
there is no comfortable position to be
where the pain will allow me sleep
fighting leaking tears uselessly.

Until the only thing I really, truly,
want with every particle of my being
is the permanent removal
of my throbbing cranium.

Notes

Love is
composed
of		feelings,
a		symphony
of			notes
arranged		together in
measures
of sweet
and sour.
Every
note is inspired
by a feeling created
within by Someone who
is gently caressing the
ivory keys of your heart.
My Someone is composing
a concert inside of me
ringing with nothing
but true beautiful
notes.

The Heart

An opulent multifaceted gemstone,
refined by the Lapidary most noble
to unveil a brilliance of pulsing light
and myriad of color ablaze with fire and life.
Birthed from a simple lump of natural rough
recognized for its potential to be tumbled
cut, abraded, ground and polished;
by passion, strength and endurance fashioned,
appraised under extreme heat and pressure.
But only the most extraordinary experience
creates the refractions necessary
to reveal true color and clarity,
organic symmetry and scintillation
amongst the shadows and inclusions
shaping uniquely identifying characteristics
flowing through the depth of the heart.

Marooned

The chain creaks and clatters
      as the anchor is raised.
I watch from a distant
      shore through the fog and haze.
You are sailing this very eve
      for places far and unknown
leaving me here on shore
      to fend for myself, alone.
When you will return
      cannot be foreseen
and by then you will have
      found another and replaced me.
The gusting wind and falling rain
      suit my mood
as your ship weighs anchor
      leaving me forever marooned.

Our Little Secret

The sunlight was brilliant.
It was perfect for a dip in the creek
once the day's harvesting was complete.
Ten years old and tickled to be in the truck,
bare legs dangling above the floorboard,
loaded to capacity and headed to the barn,
anticipating climbing in to push the beans
down the incline of the rising truck bed,
hanging on precariously for the ride
under the watchful eye of my uncle.
A pause in the forward glide
and silken strands of web are plucked
as budding fruit are fondled.
The joy in the day takes flight,
laughter dies sharp and confused,
the sun's warmth is replaced with ice,
as innocence is pinched from the tree of youth,
stolen and buried in barren soil deep.
Like poison the tarnished seeds take root
to become our little secret.

*Original watercolor painting by my
beautiful niece Sydni Strode.*

Shooting Stars

How many stars,
pure of light
and sparkly bright,
have been taken
too soon by vice
not of their choice?
Pure of soul
and amazingly gifted,
trusting innocence
manipulated,
caged and exploited,
helplessly addicted.
Lost to the scars
and lacerations
of shattered dreams.

Theology

I am
A statement of being
An individual me, self
Add two words and you have…

God
Created in his image
Every time I use this phrase
Am I claiming kinship?

Am I
Are we allowed to question?
Like a child whose response is Why?
The polar opposite of God is…

Satan

Rebirth

I arise a new child
like the young skater who
picks herself up painfully
from blade scarred ice
after another failed attempt
at a new jump, dizzy,
disappointed but determined.

I arise a new child
like the butterfly emerging
from its all encompassing
cocoon, evolved from its
lumpy larval stage, stretching
its wings to slowly launch
into ephemeral beauty.

I arise a new child
like the sinner baptized
first by fire then flooded
by the Holy Ghost after
being dumped reverently
fully clothed in a river blessed
and washed in the blood.

I arise a new child
like the Soldier who
conquered her first gun fight
in the middle of nowhere
on foreign soil knowing
band aids don't fix bullet holes
shaking and filled with life.

I arise a new child
like the T-totaler discovering
the burst of fruity flavor
and sheer enjoyment
in the relaxation of inhibitions
found in a pitcher
of green apple moscato sangria.

I arise a new child
like the survivor who
steps into open, loving arms
with the blossoming of hope,
the first threads of trust,
and loyalty found in friendship
realizing an end to violence.

Plump

Being plump is good
when referring
to a fuzzy peach.
Beautiful full lips.
Pinchable pink cheeks.
A healthy sweet baby.
But once babyhood
is left behind
plump becomes
no longer kind.
Plump becomes…
a segregator.
An isolator.
An unhealthy
self-image.

Empowering Innocence

Innocence brilliantly newborn and shining
through the eyes of a child, sparkles brightly.
Shouted in a child's voice uninhibited
by social norms, full of curiosity.
Dimmed by experience but not extinguished
if admonishment is administered
with discipline and encouragement
rather than embarrassment,
a heavy hand and self-interest.
Innocence can be strength or weakness
to be taken for granted or advantageous.
When nurtured in strength, intelligence and empathy
it manifests in joy and kindness.
When demeaned by belittlement and derision
the shine is forever tainted by self-doubt
undermined by low self-esteem
and a life long journey
seeking acceptance and approval ensues.

Shakespearean Tragedy

Who is that knocking on my door?
Why it is Life…
Come to tell me taking a pause
has its limits.
Pulling the covers over your head
is only a temporary escape
and will but make it harder
to rejoin the castaways
that are the occupants of this play…

Like so Much Detritus

I watched an empty aluminum can
forlornly gathered up and noisily
tossed by the invisible force of the wind,
clanging and bouncing along,
with no control over its destination.
Once drained of its usefulness,
having barely touched surrounding lives,
a mere shell of its original self,
it was carelessly abandoned,
becoming a hollow little shadow
overlooked until its outrage
at being so easily discarded
echoes across the parking lot
with every bumpy, noisy movement
and path altering collision.

Life's Clown

She's chasing the storm with a finial,
trying to capture raindrops in a butterfly net
while buffeted by dragon's wings on the wind
and battling its whetted fangs with a pen.

She tap dances blindly into a court room
to another's tickling of the ivories in a tune
more fitted to the swaying moves of a monsoon
working to not be swept away to the moon.

She's geared up to feed wild tigers
with an overflowing basket of wild flowers
and, stumbling on the rocks at high tide,
plummets into a safety net under the high wire.

Shattering the Wheel

Appearances were everything.
Family pictures taken annually
coordinated colors, dressed alike for unity.
The public face all smiles and amiability
proud comments and demonstrations of affection.
The repercussions for disobedience dire
and privately dispensed.
No bruises ever
at least not where visible.
Mental abuse was Her forte.
She instilled self-doubt and insecurity
with a desperate need for validation
doomed to never be satisfied.
Nothing could meet her capricious standards
leaving me feeling useless and insignificant
as stupid as She frequently declared.
All conflict attributed to my failure
regardless of the circumstances.
Indoctrinated to meekly accept blame
to be critical of every decision and action
to mistrust instincts, insights and perceptions.
Conditioned to avoid being the center of attention
through pain and humiliation
but left craving it utterly.
Instilled with the yearning to belong
but the understanding I was unworthy
I ceased to try and withdrew completely
into my own solitary world
friendly and polite but reticent.
Compliments were double edged swords
offered flippantly with insincerity
intended to hurt rather than reward.
Dad was my solace and sanctuary
my source of acceptance and praise
where I could relax and just be me
until he too betrayed me for his own safety.
Adrift until I was found, a slave to authority.
In the depths of my heart and soul He lit a flame

innate strength of my being was revealed
my worthiness to be loved illuminated.
For the first time I stood free
presented with a mirror's true reflection
purged of tarnish and misrepresentation
based on stunted jealousy.
I watched the lies vanish before my eyes
the resulting rage gave me the strength to rise
to reevaluate and sift the ashes to find myself
without fear of denigration.
He pushed me to be me
stopped me when I started to reiterate
concepts branded on my psyche
helped me find my truth, voice and confidence.
He gave me the security to amass the power
necessary to shatter the shackles
that held me prisoner
and the courage to stand adamant
when She started the cycle anew
to prevent another generation
from the suffering I knew
by turning that wheel into splinters.

Conjunction

A square peg will absolutely
fit in a round hole.
It simply must be diminutive,
the submissive in the relationship.
The converse is more easily true.
But there will always be
wiggle room,
unfilled empty space,
aloneness,
unsatisfied air,
room for individual growth.

Easter Rumination

He is risen!
Given that He died in the most excruciating way
paying for sins not His own
grown up knowing He was God's sacrificial lamb
and would descend into the very pits of Hell
enveloped in evil and wrongdoing not of His own making
hating not those whose burden He assumed
assuaging God's historical need for a sacrifice
rising on the 3rd day from the dead
demonstrating God's power and divine love for mankind.
Passage into His kingdom assured by belief in Jesus
He is risen!

He is risen!
Why? What did I contribute,
that I might benefit from this...
this ultimate act of sacrifice?
Love and devotion for a sibling,
for are we not all called God's children?
Why would a parent sacrifice one child
to save another from death and suffering?
Unless the sacrifice was willingly made?

Noah's Relief

A bright hole opens
in the inky dark clouds
allowing a single beam of sunlight
and warmth to penetrate.
Creating an awesome prism
of dazzling colors that stretches
across the horizon.
A promise fulfilled
a wondrous beacon of hope
to also see a very small
patch of blue sky and white clouds.
After 40 days and 40 nights
of dark treacherous rain.
Everything saturated
nowhere to get dry.
A ship cast astray
on the roiling ocean
with waves rising higher
than the crow's nest
sails in peril of tearing loose
in the merciless wind
isolated and alone
with only family, faith
and the two by two
God entrusted him to save.
An olive branch was delivered
and Noah weeps in gratitude.

The Magic of Christmas

Trappings and Bows

Mom always made Christmas.
Her spirit started Black Friday
with boxes of decorations and lists of wishes,
peanut brittle, cookies, fudge, and treats divine.
Flashing lights on two Christmas trees,
one filled with ornaments children created
one traditional silver, gold, pink and burgundy,
both lovingly decorated in great detail.

Christmas music rang cheerfully for weeks.
Fireplaces blazed, popped and snapped happily,
the warmth welcome to frozen toes and noses
on decorating warriors covered in snow.

Giggles rampant as we slid and coasted
to the kitchen where Mom had hot chocolate wai
with hot dogs for roasting and marshmallows for
the television tuned to play and replay
a list of Christmas favorites from Rudolph and Frosty
to the Grinch, Charlie Brown, White Christmas,
Miracle on 34th Street, a Christmas Carole, George Bailey,
and rounding out the season with the Sound of Music.

Boxes brightly wrapped in ribbons and bows,
filling the tree skirt, piled and overflowing.
Coordinating colors tantalizingly tagged and arranged,
not to be touched, in wondrous torment, until the big day.

Christmas Eve

The day always took on the glow of anticipation.
Christmas lights blinking through snowflakes,
excited giggles, shrieks and snowball impacts
creating the music of a winter holiday break
after Mom ejected us so she could accomplish
last minute gift wrapping and celebration planning.

Adorned in our color-coordinated Christmas finery
it was off to Grandma's house for dinner before church.
Spit-polished, hair curled, black patent shoes, rosy cheeks,
admonished for best behavior as Santa's watching,
and the promise of a special gift in reward
kept us compliant while excitement surged.

Christmas Eve candlelight service
is among my absolute favorite memories.
The hush over the sanctuary as the pews filled,
the carols, the choir, all lights extinguished,
then softly flickering flames bouncing symbolically
off stained glass with Jesus' light gently growing.

Bundled up on the sleepy ride home.
Bouncing awake in wide eyed excitement.
Matching pajamas finally donned
knowing Santa's arrival is imminent,
snugly tucked into bed listening for Ho ho ho…
eye lids slowly drooped into gentle rest.

The Wondrous Day

He jumps out of bed fully awake, dimples alight,
and low crawls in his best Soldier rendition
from bedroom to living room to peek at the sight
of fulfilled Christmas wishes.

Rudely awakened by a giggling, bouncing fireball
dressed from head to toe in blue footy pajamas
unfortunately, completely matching mine
grinning from ear to ear whispering animatedly.

Santa's been here, Santa's been here!!
You gotta come and look!!
Always the conservative, rule minding big sister
I remind him we have to wait or risk losing the loot.

He jumps up and down a few more times
nearly dragging me out of bed

for the forbidden excitement
of looking at what Santa has left.

An empty plate and glass with milk residue
on the octagon table next to the tree,
and a couch loaded with toys and stockings filled
with hidden surprises and sweet treats.

We tumble over each other getting to the stairs
laughing gleefully as we consider
how best to wake the parents, who are already aware
that we are awake, noisy little critters.

After fake sleeping, mumbling, and playful snores
their appearance means the baking of cinnamon buns,
sounds of joy as gifts are given and wrapping paper is torn,
the feelings of warmth, and the echoes of love.

Then, dressed in our finest play-ready clothes,
allowed to take only one of our entertainments,
it's off to Grandma's house we go
to celebrate the rest of this wondrous day.

What is Christmas?

Memories….
Large noisy wonderful gatherings
voices raised in song and laughter.
Children as both joy and holy terror
racing through the house playing tag
dodging grownups and ignoring admonishment.
Snow falling, sledding, snow forts, and snowball fights
bundled up looking like the snowman we built
big as we could with small hands and tools.
Smiles and carols and shopping
drug through the mall searching for the perfect gift.
The scent of marshmallow fudge and baking cookies
slowly permeating and drawing kids from every nook.
Busy hands in the kitchen whipping up the goodies,
with spoon fights in cookie dough quelled by Mom's LOOK.
Glowing lights and tinsel on the tree
Ornaments, each with its own special memory,
silver and gold in garlands and boughs of evergreen,
presents in colorful paper and glittery bows full of mystery,
lights blinking and doors hung with Christmas wreaths.
Dressing up in our finery for the Christmas Eve service
celebrating baby Jesus with plays, pageants and songs
remembering our Soldiers with silent prayers
and wishes for their return soon and safely.
Special gifts just for us with excitement and gladness
from Grandma and Grandpa, Mom and Dad.
Anticipation awaiting Santa with bated breath,
milk and cookies, bedtime stories, yearning to hear bells
and the sound of hooves hitting the roof as a sleigh lands.
Wonder at an empty glass and plate, a bulging sock

a new bike, a doll and a book lovingly displayed.
Allowed one new toy to take to Grandma's place.
Christmas dinner laid out crowding the countertops,
smells of ham and roasted turkey
all family favorites; sweet bread rolls, oyster dressing,
mac 'n cheese, green beans, mostaccioli, and pecan pies.
Grandma and Grandpa by the fireplace
or at the table, all heads bowed, saying grace.
Mom on the piano tickling the keys
with laughter and music entertaining
pulling a crowd and inspiring all to sing.
Ripping wrapping paper as children are released
excited exclamations and glowing faces
with echoes of "Thanks" ringing throughout the space.
The noisiness of hugs, love and joy expressed.
Finding a quiet corner hidden away for some seclusion,
after the celebration ebbs and football hits the tube,
with a new book, game or needlework tightly on a hoop.
Bundling up once again before the sleepy trip home
always the last to leave with warm wishes and hugs
bittersweet goodbyes for another Christmas has
passed and another year of memories honed…

Bells

If an angel gets its wings
every time a bell rings
then I want bells everywhere
hanging freely in the air,
so even stray little breezes
can wiggle through and release
joyous music from the bells
doing their part to facilitate
all angel fledglings
getting their guardian wings.

To Die in the Spring

To die in the Spring
after the solemnity of Lent has ended
and celebration of His resurrection is done.
That is when I want to go.

To die in the Spring
after the dripping sound of melting snow
accompanied by crackling of ice fills the air.
That is when I want to go.

To die in the Spring
after, or between, its thunderstorms
and the slow release of winter's grasp.
That is when I want to go.

To die in the Spring
when the colors are vibrant and new
and the air is filled with the scent of birth.
That is when I want to go.

To die in the Spring
after dogwood petals fall like snowflakes
and the daffodils and tulips bloom.
That is when I want to go.

To die in the Spring
after the hummingbirds arrive
and, with the bees, start raiding flowers.
That is when I want to go.

To die in the Spring
after witnessing the fawns and foals
begin to gambol about in excited curiosity.
That is when I want to go.

To die in the Spring
before the heat of summer takes hold
and the landscape starts to scorch brown.
That is when I want to go.

Service and Sacrifice

Our Flag Is Tattered

Our flag is tattered,
hanging limply.
The breath of patriots
is loud and fierce
but not enough
to lift it proudly.

Our flag is tattered,
forlornly drooping.
The country is divided
in danger of falling.
As previously warned,
it cannot stand.

Our flag is tattered,
sadly scorned.
We must return
to center, together,
to democratic balance.
Shout down extremists.

Our flag is tattered,
But open hearts can lift it.
Compassionate ears
and peaceful voices
can bring us back,
reunited as Americans.

Our flag is tattered,
but still there is hope.

A Symbol of Strength

A bald eagle with wings fully extended
flies over my left shoulder.
His shadow covers me protectively.
I understand that he will stand resolute
in my defense from all who wish me harm,
ensuring my freedom from oppression.

Windsnakes

Our chopper settles
on home ground,
sending windsnakes rushing
wildly through the grass.

Ignition switched off,
the rotors' whirling slowly dies,
life slowly sucked
from wired brain
and muscle.

Windsnakes rush wildly
through the grass.

The sides burst open
disgorging us all.
Released into freedom
we thank the Lord.

Windsnakes rush wildly
through the grass.

We remember, always,
with the guilt of survivors,
those left behind
without peace or freedom,

only bloodshed and fighting.
No rest for those
not as lucky as
we who are home.

Windsnakes rush wildly
through the grass.

We shed tears
of happiness and relief
reunited with loved ones
knowing those left
will never do
as we do now.

Windsnakes rush wildly
through the grass.

We look to our banner
of stars and stripes,
red, white and blue,
and wonder.
The war is over but
windsnakes will forever
be impressed on our minds.

Photo taken by Amanda Camden Photography

Music of an Army Base

Unison voices of physical fitness
The drum roll chatter
of Soldiers preparing for duty
Reveille
announcing the raising
of our flag with its first note
Voices raised in staccato song
to keep boots in tangent
tapping out the marching movement
Drill Sergeants' chorus shouted
in enigmatic canon
as Trainees are indoctrinated
The Army Song issuing forth
from classrooms before instruction
Mess Call
The percussion of ordnance
rattling windows in time
Blank fire in accompaniment
to the cantonment traffic
The frenetic barking of working dogs
training to save Soldier lives
The silence and stillness
that surrounds the respect shown
Retreat
The blast of the cannon on last note
preceding our national anthem
or To the Color as our flag is lowered
The raucous cacophony of Soldiers
at dinner and evening preparations
for the next duty day
Taps
The quiet that follows
the haunting horn singing out
its soulful sound as the day is done

A Generation Marked

On the blacktop between this town and the next
listening to the radio when horrible events
were set in motion... the wake-up call sent.
What an incredibly terrible accident!!
How could this have happened?
Only a few precious moments were we allowed
to continue our complacent delusion....
A second plane exploded through
another invulnerable tower.
Reality hit the airwaves like a sledgehammer
as another struck the center of national defense
and still another was foiled by actions of selfless souls
who gave their lives to protect unknown others.
A series of events that marked a generation
showcased courage and heroism
underscored and highlighted the fallacy
of the security and inviolability
believed to exist in our sacred homeland.
Haunting loss, images of tears streaked through ash
painted by evil unified a country of pioneers
willing to raise arms in defense of freedom.

*Photo taken by Amanda Camden Photography of
people looking at the Twin Towers Memorial*

Photo taken by Amanda Camden Photography

Loss of Freedom

The darkness of ignorance
walking blindly through the tunnel
self-imposed and enveloping
following misleaders trustingly
into the abyss of misinformation.
Misunderstanding willingly and with intent
indulgent self-delusion
without regret.
Relinquishing the unforgiveable
freely given without asking the fee
in defiance of those who gave all
for its procurement.
Unrecognized until it's too late to speak
too late to fight the bonds or find a cure
for the venom that flows sparkling
through the spider's sticky reaping
as it sits content with its crop
of tightly cocooned and tormented sheeples.

The Lost and Forsaken

Lost
Those who've seen and done more
than their minds can handle
in an unsanctioned war,
involuntarily sent to experience horrible atrocities.
Patriots who served their country in humid jungles
wounded physically and spiritually.
Returned home to be eviscerated,
ostracized, misunderstood, shunned, and vilified.
Experiencing loss of family and fellowship,
unsuccessfully hiding invisible scars,
unable to re-assimilate,
permanently charred by contact with evil.
Left in rags with nothing.
Considered useless vagrants and trash,
living on the streets in boxes, scavenging.
Politically unsightly, indecent, and dangerous.

Homeless
Holding onto minute mementos
of a past they can't forget or overcome;
medals received for heroism,
pictures that sustained them through the horror,
of loved ones whose acceptance was denied.
They still hear shots fired,
screams of the dying,
still see faces of those who have fallen,
those they could not save
and those held while their lives fled,
envied for the peace they would attain
beyond the awful reality that surrounded them.
Brothers in arms owed a debt
that can never be paid.

Forsaken
by a society that thought them worthless,
by the government that sent them into hell,
by families who failed them,
by themselves.

Heroes

There are those easily recognizable
military servicemen and women
who are away before dawn or out after dusk
in battle zones and on covert missions,
or called to support national and state emergencies.

There are those on four legs who fearlessly risk
to save human lives on patrol,
sniffing for bombs, drugs, contraband,
using speed, smarts, teeth and claws.

There are those who hold the blue line
answering a different call
on a different mission to protect and serve.
They may wear blue,
they may wear black,
they may wear white,
but their sirens alert all that help is imminent.
Be it protection from bodily harm,
upholding the law,
fighting fires, or saving lives.
They risk all on the streets
with no thought for self-preservation.

There are those who greet the sirens
at the Emergency Department doors
or above on the floors
selflessly, tirelessly serving to heal.

These are the obvious Heroes.

Then there are those in service to the Heroes
serving the call for self-sacrifice in a different way.
Those chair borne rangers
managing logistics, meals and pay
overseeing training, order and discipline.
Showing respect to those
who gave the last full measure of devotion.

Families who understand their Heroes'
burning need to serve, and suffer their absence
at special events and important moments,
understanding when they just want peace,
don't want to share the horror of their day,
just need to hold or be held.

Educators forming the minds of our children
to develop future leaders and Heroes,
teaching history in the hopes
past mistakes will never be repeated.

Service animals for wounded and retired
who simply bring peace with their presence,
those with a nose for seizures, cancer, and diabetes,
and who see or hear where senses have been taken.

Those who stand up when they see a wrong
and speak out in defense of the less able
whether it be with words or, if necessary,
the willingness to stand in front and take action.

Those who simply give of themselves to others
because time is a precious commodity
greatly taken for granted.
These are the less obvious Heroes.

Dog Tags

Two simple pieces of silver metal
rectangular with a folded lip,
stamped up personalized
and strung on chains.
Imbued with mystical importance
during training where they are implanted,
like an acorn stuffed in the dark fertile soil
of an impressionable, un-indoctrinated mind,
which takes root and grows into a majestic oak;
or an embryo clinging to the uterine wall
of its mother as it sucks in energy
to miraculously become something
much greater than its single celled origin,
taking on a life of its own.

Carried continuously,
a routine part of the uniform.
Onerous during daily life,
bright and shiny, cold and noisy.
Becoming reverent upon death.
Separated to ensure identification
and the return of recovered remains.
Sometimes the only thing left
to be recovered, returned to loved ones
who anxiously await news,
dreading the official notification.
They symbolize closure and, often,
relief with guilt, sorrow, tears and pride.

Their permanence a lasting reminder
to survivors, fellow service members,
dependents, descendants,
and the respectful many,
of the sacrifice of the few
for the wellbeing and way of life

of those they fought for and loved.
Cherished as a symbol of sacrifice
worn proudly, displayed or still carried,
tucked away in a jewelry box
with other service memorabilia.
Included in a memorial for a particular war
commemorating lives that went
Above and Beyond.

At a Military Funeral

Standing in a sprinkling Spring rain
surrounded by respect and grief
at the conclusion of funeral honors
for a Vietnam Veteran laid to rest.
The flag folded and presented
in great ceremony by the honor guard,
Taps played, the vault opened.
Its darkness awaiting the urn
and a seal freshly engraved
with name and rank.

Standing in the sprinkling rain
utterly shaken, emotionally invested,
I determined this Veteran will not see
the interior of a mausoleum vault.
Send me off to Valhalla in a boat aflame,
for have I not a warrior been?
Give me a Native American tree burial
that I might kiss the sky.
I want to feel the sunlight as a blade of grass,
spread my ashes at the base of an apple tree
that I might nourish my favorite fruit,
or let them drift over a swiftly flowing stream
that I might float one last time
and nurture the flora and fauna
I dedicated my life to protecting.

The Ship is Sinking

The ship's Captain is demented,
the First Mate is a useless hyena,
the Second Mate is inebriated,
the parrot is screaming about mutiny,
the crew is divided unevenly.
The minority loudest with their folly
believes the parrot's malady,
leaving the silent majority
in consternation eternal
and watching as the ship is sinking.
The lion whose roar brought peace,
supplanted by failed democracy,
waits intently for an opportunity
to trim the sails and reset
the course of the ship's journey
before a rendezvous with Davy.

Suicide Survivor

What?!? No!! Seriously?!?
Grief.
Flooding tears.
WHY??
What was he thinking??
What was going on in his life
to make this the only option?
Anger.
At anyone perceived
to have added pressure.
You. Him. Her. Them... Me.
Guilt.
More anger.
What could I have done?
I could have helped!!
Why didn't I see it??
Why didn't he let me in??
A folded flag and Taps
shreds what is left of my heart.

Midville, USA

Center of the country
but west of the Gateway
where liberals are outnumbered
by conservatives four to one.
Lost in the woods where
nothing is flat
surrounded by wildlife
interspersed with livestock
and agriculture, but only
where ridges and valleys allow.
In Midville, small town USA
you will find quiet,
slow speaking,
don't-miss-a-detail,
frequently mistaken
for dim witted,
culturally backward,
socially ignorant,
and uneducated people
who are the antithesis
of these assumptions.
Where most grew up around,
and are fluent in firearms
for sport and defense,
willing to stand up
for the principles and freedoms
on which this country
was founded.
Not willing to take a knee
in the face of tyranny
or to willingly give up
God-given rights
for a false sense
of security and providence.
Where neighbors
look out for each other
while minding their own.
Where kids are allowed
to be kids while learning
responsibility and self-sufficiency.

Teach the Children

Teach the children
and they will know only indoctrination.
Couch lessons in animation and song
and they will happily sell our rights and freedoms.
Paint their fairy tales by the light of rose colored glasses
they will clamor for fabled entitlements.
Romanticize crime and corruption in entertainment
they will identify with one and find the other mainstream.
Use racially charged epithets and denigration
and they will learn hate and distrust.
Feed them prejudice with their mac and cheese
and manifesto becomes certitude.
Encourage superiority and condescension
humility is lost and intolerance becomes accepted.
Change the meaning of words and phrases
and they will learn a different reality.
Rewrite history books skewed to a new agenda
they will never learn from the sins of the past.
Blame sins of great-great grandfathers on descendants
and they will forever perpetuate divisiveness.
Reward all regardless of performance
and forever stymie the desire for betterment.
Punish the bullied for standing up to bullies
and remove the concept of self-defense.
Undermine their self-worth
and self-doubt will keep them silent.
Engender anthropomorphism through propaganda
they will kill our ability to defend against tyranny.
Create designer medical conditions
and remove responsibility for personal choices.
Indulge their every desire
they will fail to differentiate want from need.
Fail to instill a work ethic and fiscal responsibility
they will work for nothing but feel entitled to everything.
Frustrate curiosity and obstruct investigation
they will fail to analyze or question.
Instill learned helplessness
they will follow blindly and submissively.
Allow falsified misrepresentations to go unchallenged
society and rule of law will forever be changed.

Possession

There is no breeze,
no rustling of the leaves.
The dark of night surrounds me.
The only light is the stars,
the almost full moon so large
riding the horizon afar.
The silence is uncanny,
in solitude unsettling…
but then, I am not alone.
I feel the ghosts permeating
the air I breathe.
Instigating my chattering teeth
as they sink their cold into my bones,
searing their insubstantial souls
to goose pimpled flesh not their own.

*Original painting created by my beautiful
niece Sydni Strode.*

God Is Great and Mother Nature Rocks

Spring's Emergence

Spring tears through the Snow Queen's last defiance
with an illusion of frosty, snowflake white.
Burgeoning blooms on dogwood trees,
sprinkled under the canopy of evergreens
like rice hovering over newlyweds,
photo frozen by lightning speed photography
then splashed on nature's bright canvas
among freshly leaved timber and daffodils.
Starkly standing and stoically buttressing
the pewter of overhanging cloud oppression
sundered by splintering and blinding flashes,
the trees dance to the soundtrack of drums
heralding the oncoming threat of a thunderstorm.

Arise

A phoenix splayed across the sky
emblazoned on the darkness before dawn
wings fully unfurled and unfettered
smoke tendrils like ribbons flutter and fly
milliseconds prior to immolation.
Flames flash and blind in this microcosm
leaving only ash strewn across the aethyr
as momentary evidence of its majestic presence
before settling on the distant horizon
magically renewed in mythical rebirth.

Stalking the Sun

Tiger, tiger burning bright
dancing across the early morning sky
stalking upon the rising sun
stealthy and silent as She awakens

Tiger, tiger better be warned
though you glow brilliantly in the dawn
your ferociousness is no competition
for the fire She's about to unleash

Note: A reference to William Blake, "The Tyger"

Spring's Explosion

Spring is...

Yellow
as the bright sunlight,
fuzzy chicks and daffodils.

Blue
as the clear pastel sky.

Gold
as the Spring Gold forsythia
warms the lingering winter air.

Green
as the new grass and budding leaves.

Pink
as the redbud, catalpa,
and peony blossoms.

Purple
as the crocus, violets and irises.

White
as newborn lambs, dogwoods flowering,
and fishermen's grins.

Gray
as the storms that bring May flowers.

Silver
as the flash of mirror
from a convertible with top down.

The Lady's Vanity

Like a lady of the night, she emerges
from behind the shadowy clouds
showcasing pure, white, luminous skin
through curtains of thick raven hair.
Dominating her world every long night
watching....
Sashaying across the dark sky
she sees everything, knows everything,
omniscient....
But what is she waiting for?

Snow White's stepmother
used a mystical mirror.
Superficial truth and ephemeral answers
replaced over time.

The beauty of the Lunar Queen eclipses
all in the world below.
She need not worry.

Spring's First Flower

I am a flower
in the crystalline snow
under a sun-filled clear blue sky.

My face is upturned
to accept your blessing.

Fill me, O Lord,
with your glowing energy,

hold off the overcast
and stormy gray clouds,

that I may unfurl
my rose-tipped petals
and show that Spring is nigh.

Photo taken by Amanda Camden Photography

Photo taken by Stephanie Nutt

Dogwoods in Spring

You can't see the forest
for the dogwoods in bloom.
Like ghostly figures
scattered throughout
fluttering in the wispy wind.
Limbs hovering over the ground
covered with large white clouds
of blossoms swaying and bouncing.
Like an intervention of snow in Spring
the petals gravitate
floating to the earth
filling the air like snowflakes
at the mercy of the currents
creating an atmosphere both hazy
and delightfully fragrant.
In a blink white is replaced
by the green of leaves
slowly yet triumphantly unfolding
and the trees once again
come back into focus.

Dance of the Peacock

Anointed by the flames of Sunna
lapis, violet, and emerald are incinerated
by crimson, gold and vibrant salmon
as the peacock dances for his chosen.
Tail feathers fully fanned and bristling
spectacularly prismatic
majestically displaying his assets
with unabashed pride in glorious seduction.
Arrogantly assured of her choice
his fabulous fan of feathers slowly descends
and is dragged carelessly
like the flaming train on a wedding dress
as he leaves the brilliant stage.

Spring's Comedy

Grass is growing
winds are blowing
flower petals riding high
as clouds scoot across the sky.
A storm is rushing this way
with thunder, lightning and rain.
Hunker down little flowers
cover up and cower
but only for a blink
as the sun will shortly wink.

Kiss of the Summer Queen

Daffodils are dancing,
      Redbuds are popping
            Dogwoods are bursting,
      Crocus are crouching
Magnolias are emerging,
      Roses are budding
            Peonies are peeking,
      Hyacinths are swaying
Tulips are blooming,
      Irises are coming
            Dandelions are forming,
      Grass is growing,
The warmth of Titania's kiss
      Precedes the hummingbirds,
            Butterflies and bees buzzing.

Catching Fireflies

A child's summer diversion
from so many years ago,
not pondered in a very long time.
It strikes me as I gaze out
into the dusk before twilight,
and realize I see very few
representative blinks of light.

They were everywhere
flashing, flitting and floating.
We chased them with a child's glee
until we had a jar full blinking
brighter than a Christmas tree
covered in white twinkle lights.
Echoes of laughter fill my memories.

I reach out into the fading light
offering my hand as a perch
to a hovering firefly nearby.
It rests its wee wings for a moment
then once again takes flight
to continue on its journey
into the deepening night.

A slight breeze brushes my cheek
and chills run down my back.
With nostalgia and worry deep
in my heart and mind
I am struck by a realization.
Simple pleasures from my childhood
are disappearing from our society.

Autumn

Driving the highway
windows down
hair wickedly whipped everywhere!!
The chill of the wind on my shoulders
countered by the warmth of the sun.
Watching the hummingbirds taper off
from summer's frenzied feeding.
Colors explode,
vibrantly flaming to life
in crimson, burgundy, and gold
then falling, floating on breezes,
tossed around like ships on a raging sea.
Crisp mornings with dew-heavy grass
to crunchy frost like glazed buttercream
on a wedding cake, then
bleeding into sunshiny hot afternoons.
The scent of wood smoke of an evening
as fireplaces fire up for winter's cold.
Homecoming with weenies and s'mores,
eyes glowing in the firelight,
marshmallow covered hot chocolate
caramel flavored coffee
or cinnamon spiced apple cider
between mittened hands.
Harvesters from dawn to dusk
hauling in nature's bounty
racing to beat the storms.
Apple dunking, pumpkin carving,
squash roasted and drowned
in butter and brown sugar.
Witches, ghosts, goblins and ghouls
glide from house to home
entreaties for treats echo
as children bargain and barter
to stave off naughty tricks
involving toilet paper and drippy eggs.
Heads bowed giving thanks
for fellowship and food
kicking off the feast in celebration
of God's gifts for the year.

Photo taken by Amanda Camden
Photography

Winter's Majesty

Snowflakes are falling.
Large, fat, fluffy flakes,
like dandelion fuzz caught in a summer breeze,
floating, drifting, flying, whipped along lazily.
Sparkling crystals tossing darts of light
making your head rock side to side
to catch all the colors, sharp and bright,
surrounding you in the stark white.
Struck still in wonder and admiration of nature's majesty,
giggling silenced in a moment of awe and utter beauty!!
Piles begin to build from a lacey dusting
on all surfaces where snowflakes will stick.
Layer upon layer on fir, maple and oak… bending branches.
Also on the ground, fence, car, railings on porches,
the bird bath and feeders in the garden,
the picnic table and summer benches.
The squirrel and the Cardinal perched in the evergreen
both lightly covered from nose to tail and beak to flight feathers.
Flowers safely blanketed and sleeping
buried until the siren's call of Spring.
If awe holds you overlong
or to snowmen, snow angels and snowballs you are drawn,
the application of broom and laughter it will take
before Mom will allow entry to the hot chocolate that awaits!!

Ice on the Rose

There is ice on the rose,
glistening in bright sunlight
not warm enough to mold
and melt the frosty rime.

It magnifies the beauty within,
intensifying the bold red shade
while casting prismatic brilliance
in eye-piercing, shattering shards.

Like a stiletto to your heart,
while your eyes flood,
cloven in two helpless parts
left to bleed life's blood.

There is ice on the rose,
beware Mother Nature's beauty
for it captivates your woes
In its divine duality.

Painting the Morning

I watched through the fog over the bridge
as God cleaned the acrylics from his brush
on the canvas of the morning sky.
Broad, bold, horizontal strokes
from burgundy to pink into purple.
In amazement I observed His power
as the colors transformed
into vibrant glowing reds and golds.
The sharp edges of the brush strokes
blurred and softened into clouds
as it released His final colors.

Aurora's Awakening

Peeking over the distant darkened tree line,
like a child giggling from her hiding place
during a game of hide and go seek,
the glowing yellow orb shyly flashes its tresses,
burnished gold to copper with the growing light.
A pink blush colors the cheeks of the sky
as the celestial crescent takes her diamonds
and self-indulgently glides over the horizon.
Blue goldstone eases into amethyst then tanzanite
surrounded and imprisoned by the clear
pale icy blue topaz of an endlessly cloud free sky.
Her breath warms the air as she announces "I'm here!"

Victorian Sunrise

"Why thank you kindly, fine Sir,"
said the Sun to the pale Moon
as She rose demurely in the east
from her refreshing sleep
winking Her cloud-hooded eye
gold and demure,
blushing from pink to scarlet.
The Moon gave a gentlemanly
tip of the top hat
and, with a suggestive smirk,
boldly offered outrageous flattery
as he slowly set to the west.

The Sun's Rebirth

The sky is all grays
smoky pinks
and reds
in the steam and flames
rolling off the sun
as it is extinguished
by the western oceans,
only to rise
like the Phoenix
from the watery ashes
of its demise.

Photo taken by Steve Miller

A Winter Sunset

The sun is going down
like a fire opal cupped
in the hand of God,
casting an amber glow
over the winter woodland,
sparking off ice-tipped trees
like a Christmas tree strung
with tiny white diamonds
that flash patternlessly.
Soon the full moon
will be glaring through moving
shadows on an icy landscape.
Stars will layer infinitely
in the velvety blackness,
galaxy after Milky Way.

The Red Dragon

Taillights weave sinuously
following the road in front of me
like a red dragon in a
Chinese New Year parade.

I realize I'm part of the weave
taking my place in the continuity
as the dragon's red blazes the pre-dawn sky
heralding the sun's fiery arrival.

Preparing to Dance

Her Majesty the Sun
adorned herself in milky pink opals
over pale blue satin
in preparation for her dance
with Evening.

Dragon's Precedence

The Sun's familiar
is released into the sky
to trumpet Her Majesty's
impending arrival.

Fiery breath disperses
shadows and darkness
crackling the dawn into
a glorious prismatic display.

Reptilian tail whips the wind
furiously creating currents
transporting her announcement
silently in ever lightening ripples of color.

A Dragon's Sunset

A dragon breathing fire
across the evening sky,
Harry's Horntail hovers overhead
wings extended riding the jet stream
with gaze glaring, glowing golden
as the sun fulfills her revolution.

Note: A reference to J.K. Rowling, "Harry Potter and the Goblet of Fire".

Lunar Grace

Mistress Moon regally exits
the early morning's sky,
midnight blue curls swaying,
diamond adornments flashing,
a plethora of magenta ruffles
cascading over clouds in her wake.
Her subtle luminosity a precursor
to the Sun's radiant glory.

Tempestas' Theater

Heavy storm clouds fill the sky
hanging over the horizon
like a velvet curtain defining
the stage for a screenplay on life.

Opaque misty white fog rises
off a flowing ribbon of river,
wrapping the tops of verdant trees,
following folds, dips and crevices
in the earth's intricate raiment.

Whistling winds twine through the script
like musical compositions issuing
from the hollow of the orchestra pit,
their variability chaotic.

The sun peeks around the curtain,
fringe brushing rays that furtively escape,
freed by a stolen moment of emergence.
Eerily oppressive
       Surreally beautiful
           Intensely Technicolor.

Photo taken by Troy Kite

Daybreak

Crystalline drops in the spider's surprise
capture the first rays of golden sunlight
and toss them at me, as sharp
as a diamond throws its fiery sparkle.
I stand on the old barn's threshold
beholden....
waiting for events to unfold.
A floating visitor moves through the air
as dancing dew drops land in my hair.
The sun gently rises as the cock crows.
Giving me the light I need to notice
squirrels bounding from tree to tree
and rabbits chewing quietly,
watchfully....
on growing garden greenery.
I realize what I was waiting to see.
Life stands still and serene
while everything continues around me.

Photo taken by Kathy Rowland from Captiva Island, FL, with the assistance of Christy Stevenson Sipes

A Rainbow

The sun is shining, blinding me,
as the rain pounds my windshield
in huge splattering drops,
the wipers in continuous motion,
light also glaring off of wet pavement.
In front the sky is bright white with puffy clouds,
behind is the darkness of a thunderstorm.
I turn a corner and framed by clouds and ink
is God's promise to Noah
a vibrant spectral prism of color.

God's Doorstep

The sun sinks slowly over the horizon
silhouetting the far off mountain peaks.
Stars begin to sparkle in the sky
darkening overhead as I watch silently.
The radio is playing softly in the car
as I slowly drink my beer.
Open desert unfolds from the edge of town
and the wind whips through the hotel,
general store and saloon.
The desolate buildings allow the wind,
and his friend, Dust,
entrance through empty windows,
cracked frames, rotting old wooden planks
that make up the now dingy gray walls,
and through open doorways
that have stood empty what seems forever.
The graveyard of this antiquated cow town
sits out here forgotten and rundown.
The weeds have risen high
over the tombstones still standing.
Few of the crudely written lines

are yet visible to searching eyes.
Others have long since succumbed
to the ravages of Mother Nature.
Some say it's lonely out here at night,
but I disagree.
Peace and beauty pervade.
The friendly silence permeates the air
and is sustained by the feeling
of my grandfather watching
through the eyes of the ancient buildings.
I feel my grandmother's voice singing
as the breeze lightly kisses my cheek.
My ancestors move to greet me from their
eternal rest in the rustle of the tall grasses.
Their laughter is carried to me in the sound
of the rushing tumbleweeds,
their presence is felt in night's darkness.
I sit alone on my car with just the radio
and sounds of the night creatures
to keep me company while I think.
Out here God's whispery voice
can be heard in the wind that blows
from those far-off mysterious mountains.
Only here can I hear His soft answers
to the questions beating in my heart,
resounding through my lonely soul
as I move through life.
Lonely I may be,
but never truly alone,
especially not when I am here,
on God's doorstep.

Illusory Mountains

Routine made surreal,
the comfortable slightly unnerving.
God's power voiced through
Mother Nature's hand
in the lightening darkness
of pre-dawn.
The clouds in the eastern sky
dense and heavily hanging
on the horizon showcasing
the sliver of moon surrounded
by stars above
creating the illusion
of driving into the mountains
where none should exist.
Halos around lights
and road signs intensified
in the barest of fog
layering the ground
making the familiar strange.
My heartbeat increases
at the beauty of the colors.
Striations stain the clouds
enhancing the illusion
of rock formations ahead
as they climb to the heavens.
Using shadow for crevices
brightness peeking through
for highlights.
The familiar becomes unfamiliar
giving pause to seamless
motion and the rise
of imaginary obstacles.

A Spring Storm

Rain, Rain…
please lighten up
and just drench everything.

There's no need
to gully wash,
and then run away…

River's Solitude

Ripples encircle the burbling spring
as it rises from its source deep underground,
drifting wider and wider, until they are washed
downstream by the currents of the river.
A cooling mist hangs above the turbulence,
droplets creating prismatic rainbows
with the sunlight while easing the heat.
Bees buzz, dragonflies flit and butterflies float
on the breeze caressing my sun heated cheek,
fish break the surface, launching themselves
in a challenge to the ambient air, and lose to gravity,
turtles sunbathe on logs and rocks serenaded
by nearby bullfrogs, oblivious of my presence.

Photo taken by Steve Miller

Hummingbirds #2

Wings blurred in motion
Needle bills plunged deep
Flitting joyfully
In competitive dance

Levitation over blooms
Radiant iridescence
Darting hibiscus to rose
Breathtaking acrobatics

Ruby throats flashing
In nature's splendor
Rose to hydrangea
Delight in motion

Spider's Weave

How beautiful are the webs woven
by spiders, brightly colored or shaded brown,
held hostage by the fickle whim
of a leaf or branch at the will of the wind?
Strands break loose whipping wildly
tearing free to fly away like a waif
slipping sinuously unseen through a crowd.
Hours of single-minded effort wiped
from existence within a flash or wink.
Tenacity takes tenuous steps toward
reconstruction as the spider drops on new wire
spinning anew the same, but different, weave.
A bridge line is tossed on the same wind
that absconded with the previous lacework,
spinnerets creating and guiding the silken flow.
Anchors fabricate an elegant framework
to support the silk as the spider imposes the warp
over which will be intertwined the sticky spiral filling
devising the trap on which the spider will wait.

Photo taken by Markus Spiske

Innocence of the Rose

As it breaks free of the seed and escapes the soil
reaching for the warmth of sunlight glowing yellow
the rose does not ponder its birth, nor does it wonder
how many days with which it will be blessed
before winter withers away its glamour.

The rose does not question as its branches
flourish and multiply green with thorns,
clothed in leaves riding gently, but provocatively,
every breeze borne by each graceful length,
its terminus graciously displaying the pinnacle
of its existence in fabulous color.

Am I beautiful?

Its bounty offered unselfishly to bees and hummingbirds
that they may feast and buzz or bounce fitfully
from bud to bloom unknowingly participating
in life's mating rituals carrying pollen pistol to stamen
in the glorious dance of propagation
to facilitate life after death.

The bud of its final bloom bursts forth
opening ever so slowly, its wealth of petals
flirting shyly with Mother Nature's buzzing
and chirping little midwives,
only to wither and die in an infinitesimal blink.

Its dazzling raiment starts to dim and brown
as temperatures start steadily down
after the blazing heat of summer months.
Still the rose does not count its final moments.
The slinking encroachment of dormancy
takes it into the unknown, or unremembered,
darkness of death and seasonal rest,
followed by the echoing question…

Am I still beautiful?

Spirits of the Roads' Remains

Shadows frolic and float
ghosts trailing an eerie aura
alongside the lonely road.
Seen only in the glowing

or dimming of barely light
in early morning or late twilight.

Animals they are,
hit by passing cars.

Continually reliving
the moment of their awful demise,
the needle at the end of the record
scratching repetitious with white noise.

Gruesome to see them hovering
over the carcasses of their remains.

Deer, dogs, rabbits, raccoons, turtles…
Armadillos, opossum, cats, squirrels…

Then there are the raptors
caught in a flying loop
impact, catapult and loose feathers
left rolling with beak askew.

Those who care, sorrow and see,
can, with a heartfelt prayer, release

these ghostly earthbound spirits,
begging mercy for lack of consideration

shown to creatures great and small,
and commending them to God's keeping
for He gave a soul to all
despite man's attempts to deny.

As God is man's shepherd
so too are we engendered

as guardians to watch over
all who call this world home.

Fur-Babies Make Us Better Humans

Freaky Feline Frolicking

Everyone felt euphoric
for fish was on the bill of fare.
Feline faces fastidiously framed
by fish-free whiskers and fur.
Bathing complete and feeling frisky
flying freely throughout the house
expending freaky feline effervescence
with frenetically flipping tails.
Followed by freedom from noise
as furry piles form for forty winks.

Picture provided by Steve Miller

Patchwork Heart

If pictures could be taken,
depicting in full color cross-section,
the gaping holes left in my heart
by the untimely departure
of beloved furry companions and friends
a miraculous vision would be presented.

Where there should be unsightly pits
God has lovingly stitched little paw prints
after filling each crater
with love and joyful memories,
overstuffing each so full
that the stitches stretch and pull.

Each paw print shaped patch is adorned
with a special name or endearment
giving the illusion that my ticker
is an unfinished patchwork quilt
ever growing, warm and comforting
expanding with each new patch and stuffing.

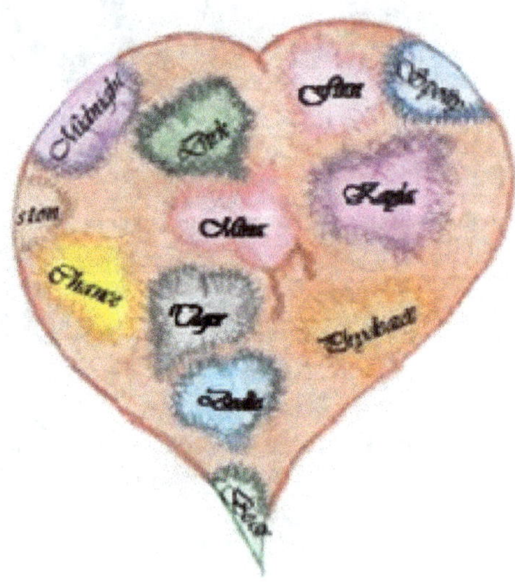

Loss of a Furry Friend

Of course, it hurts when they leave us
for the very last thing they do
is wrap their ghostly paws
around the shattered bits of your heart
and force them all back into place
tethering them tighter to your soul.
Except for that one little piece
they claim for themselves,
taken like a child's blanky
or favorite stuffed toy,
to keep them warm in your love,
to comfort them in your absence,
and to make it easier to find them
when it is time to be reunited.

Kayla's Song

My best friend died today
the Lord took her away.
It happened so suddenly
leaving me aching and lonely.
I miss her smile and sparkling eyes,
her love and passion for life.

Her mere presence brought
warmth to my heart
light to my spirit
laughter to my life and
joy to each day.

Her joy in seeing me was always there,
she had to follow me everywhere.
Happy kisses and wagging tail
always ready to run and play
with her ever present toy to chase,
just in case....

Her devotion brought
forgiveness to my soul
selflessness to my actions
patience to my inner self and
comfort to my sadness.

She had great pointy ears
to listen to my sorrows and fears.
A big furry warm body
on cold days to keep me company.
An impressive bark and snapping bite
used in play to display her might.

She brought me
compassion

companionship
faithfulness and
unconditional love.

Lymphoma extinguished her beautiful light
and forced me to take her life.
I guess her last lesson for me
was the importance of mercy.
I always thought, as a puppy, we rescued her
but now I am not so sure.

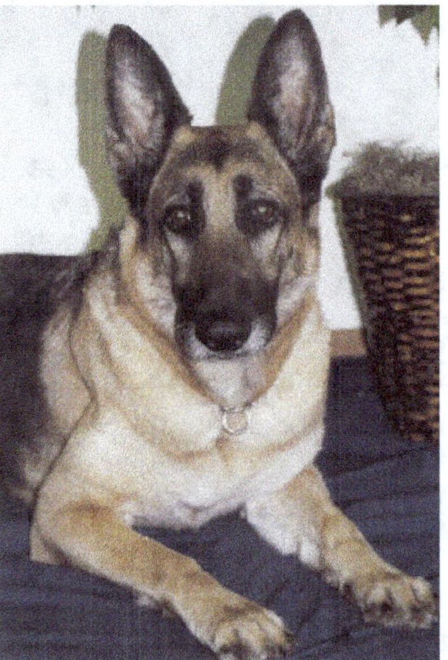

Photo taken by Sarah Pehlman

Ode to Chance

My friend is arriving on the wings of angels.
Will You look after him until I get there?
He's a loving companion and beautiful friend,
with his pointy ears and toothy grin,
his warm heart shining in his big brown eyes,
his tail wagging in happy times.
He likes his ears and tummy scratched
and will chase anything you throw to catch.
His ball is his favorite toy,
with it we shared much laughter and joy.
He makes a wonderfully warm fur blanket,
and sings beautifully with the right music.
He willingly cleans ears, toes, noses and fingers
with an enthusiasm that lingers.
He is very patient and will wait for you,
forever if you need him too.
He is very quiet and unobtrusive
sometimes you will forget he is with you.
His time with me has enriched my life
his goodness has inspired me to strive
to be worthy of his love and devotion
ultimately, to be a better person.

Leading the Way

I miss you today and I'll miss you tomorrow
my heart is filled with sorrow.
My best friend and constant companion
looked up at me with pain filled eyes.
She is exhausted just by standing
and moves to a spot nearby where she can lie
but still see me as I move around.
Normally glued to my side she would be
with joy and anticipation
for the toss of the toy I always have with me.
But not today
   Today is the day
     she has told ME to stay
       It's time for her to go away
         to find the end of the rainbow
           where no physical pain can follow
             and even though my heart is hollow
               I know she needs to hear "free dog" so she can go…
I miss you today, I'll miss you tomorrow
my heart is ever filled with sorrow.
I thank God for every minute of every day
for giving me the gift that was your love and loyalty,
for sending you my way,
for the bond that made us a family.
You had the heart and drive to help
those lost in the wilderness
your nose would lead us to the rescue
until you saved the day there was no rest.
But not today
   Today is the day
     we put her toys away
       no more will she show us the way.
         She deserves a respite from the pain
           where she can be whole again
             a soft spot in the sun where she can lay
               awaiting my arrival so we can play…
I miss you today, I'll miss you tomorrow
my heart is still filled with sorrow
but I know where she goes, I will follow.

Photo taken by Gary Nall. Dedicated to Gary Nall and his K9, Neeva, whose life and career in Wilderness Search and . Rescue was tragically cut short

Photo taken by Greg Horn. Dedicated to Greg Horn in remembrance of Asta, a wonderful friend and great working dog. She touched many more lives than we probably understand just by being who she was.

She Was So Much More….

She was my companion.
She was my friend.
She was my partner.
She was my heart.

She was the last chosen, too timid,
her potential was doubted.
She needed understanding and patience,
encouragement and acceptance,
which I gave unreservedly,
as did she.

She had determination and heart,
she had drive and smarts.
She loved to play, as any dog does,
but her play saved Others.

She was a Working Dog.
Her game was finding the lost,
her reward a Kong and "good girl",
she worked because I asked it of her.
Our bond created an unbeatable team
because she placed her trust in me.

She was my validation,
when needed, my consolation.
She was my confidant.
She was my gift.

Now that my partner is gone
I'm the one who is lost.
Without her I'm somehow lessened,
floating aimlessly,
disconnected from those around me
as if she was my tie to humanity.

She made me whole.
She had her paws in my soul.
She was so much more…
than just a dog.

Disaster Training Wash-Out

The runt of the litter and all that was left
you came with doggie baggage.
Told on the ride home repeatedly
be cute, suck up to Mommy and beg.
Poor little malingator was so exhausted
the next two weeks you spent
quietly sleeping on Mommy's chest.

But then you and Dad started training
a disaster SAR dog you would be.
Your true personality took the reins
and with your hydraulic butt you were revealed
to be hardheaded, stubborn and temperamental
with selective hearing, but mysteriously endearing
winning every female heart you encountered.

When Dad took you to disaster camp he decided,
because the job requires ears, nose and drive,
no exceptions every time,
even K-9 bonded you were not reliable
because you generally left one or another behind.
But when all were there and on line,
good you looked and the victim you would find.

So our irritating, astonishing, beloved pet you became
assuming your new role with ease
in your own fascinating way.
Lovingly you were renamed Richard Cranium
when your doggie baggage was put on display.
Then Queen Bee made her entrance on the scene
and your heart was whisked away.

Over the years health issues manifested
and you would flag then rally
amazing us with your resiliency.
You beat Lyme's and (we thought) thyroid disease
making us believe you'd live forever,
giving us a false sense of security
to lose you, so many times we were prepared.

More wrong we could not have been.
When the time truly arrived,
heartbroken, Mommy felt you take your last breath
the Pit Bull cried
and the world shifted on its axis.
But you went out as you lived, your terms, your time.
Swiftly and dramatically, we were bereft
leaving only memories behind.

Your tug toy, squeaker and a ball.
Your bounding up and down the hall.
Your cold nose to say I will not be ignored.
When sleeping, your woofing and snores.
The way you followed Queen Bee all over
and cleaned her ears through the crate door.
Jumping on the couch and flopping your head in a lap
The only one safe on your bed with the cats.
Growling and grumbling when touched while drinking
but sitting in puzzlement when the petting desisted.
Searching for Mommy when she's away on a trip...
welcoming me home with a bark, head bump and a lick,
those big soft brown eyes looking into mine.

We are more having loved you
and loved you so much we let you go
letting your spirit loose
to go where only you know
strong, beautiful and true
to ride the everlasting rainbow.

My Recycled Fur-Baby

Incomprehensible it is to me
that another would place so small a value
on such a gentle creature
as the sweet quiet little you
who stumbled into my life
That they would toss you away like
yesterday's useless refuse,
leave you behind as they moved away,
unknowing and uncaring for your well-being.
Starving, shivering and in the motherly way
ragged, malnourished and covered in dirt
with this round unmistakable girth,
you crawled out of hiding
at the sound of my approach
looking only for kindness,
companionship and a gentle touch.
You found a soft welcoming heart,
a full belly and a warm hearth.
You, my recycled fur-baby,
found a new home and safety.
Timely it was for thee
as the very next day
my Birkenstocks became "birthing-stocks"
for six brand new little sparks.
New homes were found
loved and spoiled the sparks will be.
Except we were bound
to go from one to three.
We couldn't part with two of your little sparks
who absconded with our hearts!!

Mina

I no longer have to hide my little green pillow
and my stuffed elephant is nicely displayed.
No longer will they be victimized by doggie slobber
or become chew toys with rips and tears
because they smell like Mommy,
or remind you of your first fleecy squeaky bear…
the one Daddy rewarded you with during
puppy rubble training,
given in a game of tug
so proud you found your victim.

What I wouldn't give to have slobber on my pillow,
to walk in and catch you with my beanie
in the middle of the bed,
to hear Daddy laughing at your shenanigans,
to feel your furry body snuggled up to me
as I drift off to sleep,
to awaken with your head on my pillow
your fur tickling my nose,
or your back to mine and your feet
pushing Daddy off the bed.

What I wouldn't give to be on the couch
your head in my lap,
bumping my elbow with your nose
every few seconds
because I'm ignoring you
as I try to surf the Internet.
Up, twirl, slapping me with your tail,
raking the cushions to get them just right
then flopping like a ton of bricks.
I'd laugh rather than scold, I promise,
to hear the sigh of contentment that would follow.

Your beautiful silky pointy ears,
so soft and warm.
Your golden amber eyes sparkling with life.
That cold wet brown nose shockingly well placed.
Grinning that self-assured doggy grin
knowing you are loved
and can do no wrong.

Oh, how I miss my beautiful baby girl.

A Puppy's Entrance

Darkness the only constant
when watery warmth and harborage
are suddenly stripped asunder.
First felt is Cold…
cold cold cold… and wet… and shivering.
Then an abrasive but loving touch
brings gentle comfort as itty bitty grubber
is washed dry from tail to whiskers.
Scent is realized with whimpering wonder
bathing every nerve ending
in strange uncomfortable vibrations.
Mama… warmth, fur and… Food!!
as the little wiggle worm,
realizing the ability to move,
latches onto the nearest nipple
and chugs to a full belly
then it's nap time for an exhausted puppy.
Only moderately disturbed when joined
by another… and another… and another…
Weightlessness and motion
as Mama's humans snag a snuggle
wiggle, whimper and weakly wail
until her tongue affirms safety
then it's new smells to catalog.
Light assaults more nerve endings
blazing blinking brightness
suddenly surrounded by BLUE
as eyes slit open and view the world
through distorted astonishment.
Everything encountered viewed
with trepidation and hesitation
until confidence is built, curiosity kindled.
Then it's pounce and play,
tug of war with the blankey,
tail discovered and chased,
clambering over. and under. siblings
and the mountain that is Mama
until she needs a break.

Hey!!
Where did she go?
Finally able to reach the top edge
of the big blue barrier barring the way
breaching with two paws and a nose
to observe the other side.
Wow, what a great big world
that needs to be conquered!!
Hmmm…. maybe tomorrow as big yawns
announce it's once again nap time.
The puppy pile already growing
beckons and whispers seductively...
The world awaits with bated breath
for Lady Chaos to venture out and explore.

*Written for Heather Hamilton, Abe
Weahkee,, Henry and Kai to commemorate
their 1st litter of pups, July 2019.
Photo provided by Heather Hamilton.*

The Battle Lost

The fight is over.
The warrior that you were
fought valiantly.
The warriors that we are
fought by your side,
and often fought with you,
in our efforts to save you.
Our prayers went unanswered.
Hope renewed and dashed
as you continued to rally and fail,
a little farther from recovery
with each falter, a little sicker.

Your loss was unthinkable
and then simply unbearable.

Evidence still remains
in various locations…
the log of your activity
and functions, your treatment
scientifically and completely captured
still beside the bed
next to the pen you played with,
a small carrier with blanket
left sitting and uncleaned,
needles, tubing, syringes, fluids
and medicines strewn
around our pseudo treatment table,
Cans, bottles, bags and bowls
everywhere from anything
we thought might tempt you to eat.

The fight is over.
The warrior that you were
fought valiantly.
Your last act an expression
of affection and acceptance.

Heat Stroke

Did it haunt you the way it haunts me?
The image branded on my psyche
of the horror witnessed,
resulting from obvious neglect.
Failure to safeguard and ensure
the basic care and wellbeing
of a beloved escape artist, chained for his safety,
who became entangled on a scorching hot day
unable to reach his water or shade,
wearing a heavy fur coat, he couldn't evade
the heat of the sun and slowly roasted.
A slow and excruciating way to go.
Found too late to save
you scooped him up and ran, also too late,
trying to get him to a vet and medical care.
He waited for you to come to his aid
but he died in your arms on the tailgate
after flailing his head around in distress.
So utterly heartbreaking still, so many years later,
this scene plays like a movie, his pathetic flailing,
his tongue hanging out so dry and pale,
his movements weak and failing.
He struggled until there was only lethargy.
Did it haunt you the way it haunts me?
The good memories are eclipsed
by the absolute horror of this scene.

Music Ignites the Soul

The Fire in My Soul

Music lit the fire in my soul
keeps my body in constant motion.
My knee bouncing and toes tapping
to the beat of everything around me
whether electric guitar and drums
with vibrations causing my skin to hum,
boot stomping or do-si-doing
to dueling fiddles or banjos,
A cappella voices harmonizing
in wondrous epiphany;
the gently blowing wind
accompanied by birds singing,
water dancing with the current
over stones in a burbling streamlet,
surrounded by leaves brushing
and grass rustling
with crickets and buzzing wings;
or the rhythm of my heart beating
in tune with a creaking rocking chair,
the sweet snores of a beautiful bairn,
and a lullaby softly filling the air.
Music can lift me to the heavens
or cast me into the deepest darkness
constrict my chest with joy or pain
make tears fall like Spring rain
or dry them as if the tracks on my cheeks
are a false testament to emotion.
Music can incite laughter
augment excitement or terror
be a cause for introspection
or the need to take action.
It is as necessary as air,
as necessary as water,
as necessary as sustenance
for imagination and existence,
fueling the mind and the heart.
The flames ignite the sparkle in my eyes,
the welcome and sass in my smile,
the ever-present passion
that colors my every action.
Music lit the fire in my soul
filling every fracture and making me whole.

Symphony of Silence

Listen to the blissful measures of silence.
Is there ever truly an absence of sound?
In the absolute stillness just before a thunderstorm
there is still the wind shivering through the silvery leaves
brushing goose bumps over skin, ruffling clothes,
invisible fingers feathering through hair and tickling your nose,
magnificently shattered by the flash of lightning and thunder's crescendo.

Snuggled into bed during the deepest sleepless night's restlessness
chirping crickets, cicadas, sounds of scurrying critters resonating
barking of the neighbor's dog startled by movement or shadow
rhythmic clicking of the fan pull bounced by turning blades
soft shifting and sigh of a sleeping loved one's dreams
treble humming of the motor on the refrigerator initiating
infernal monolithic tone pulsing in your ears in the absence of all else.

Blessed soothing silence sought to hear one's own thoughts
calming internal dissonance and fugue following times of strife
allowing for the a cappella purge of grief and flow of tears of sadness
room to breathe and ruminate without the soul-searing judgment of others
healing balm applied generously to broken dreams
the advent of new avenues of adventure through self-imposed soul searching
finding the silver embossed lining in prelude to a new passage.

Mountainous weight of silence filling a room like slithering slime
awaiting words longed for or hated, that need, want, have to be said.
Overpowering tension of turmoil grave but also glissando
stridently straining toward a harmony easing the symphony's movement
toward an interlude of peace, modulation and lassitude.
Silence to recharge, restructure, reshape the passion
and desire to reenter the reoccurring motifs of life's sonata.

Peaceful, blissful, unbroken intermezzo of silence
integrated into the beat and flow, allegro and adagio, seamlessly
of every composition surrounding the audience encased behind glass,
held separate for an enharmonic interval of joyful selfishness.
Renewal, refreshing restful indulgence manipulated and orchestrated.
The intentional pause in the choral presentation of God's presents
listening to blissful measures of silence.

A Cappella

Music was the light in my eyes,
the sparkle glimmering in my soul,
as necessary as ice cream to the sugar addict.

To raise my voice in song was
cold fresh water on a parched throat,
air to a freediver attaining 300 meters,
Mama's cooking after an 18 month deployment.

Music was me painting in creative color,
bathing loved ones in beauty and emotion,
wrapping the world in a ribbon of my joy,
like effervescent pink Champaign bubbles
or… yellow cocktail music.

I barely sing in a whisper now
and never with the abandon of the unaware,
my range diminished as that of the wild buffalo,
shrinking like the rain forest,
fading with the diamond's creation,
sacrificed in the volcano's flow.

Music

It washes over me like an unstoppable wave
enveloping, all encompassing, captivating,
scouring every crevice and wrinkle clean
of weariness and bone deep worries
to the very tips of fingers and toes.
It's a balm to the troubled and tormented soul,
evocative memories weave through its wake
rippling and wrapping around your brainstem,
intermingling warmth and emotion overwhelming
until cathartic saltwater unleashes further cleansing.

It envelops me like dryer warmed fleece,
softly draped, covering from nose to tootsies,
insulating, if only momentarily, from the icy reality
that accompanies daily responsibilities,
that tunnel solutions and fog perceptions.
Liquidly flowing as hot chocolate to every cell
after hours of snowmen, igloos and snow angels.
A reminder of childhood pleasures carefree and secure,
times personally formative and traditionally momentous
surrounded by absolute certainty and love.

It encompasses me like an unexpected hug,
unsolicited, impulsive, given unconditionally
with joy and innocence, unknowingly answering
an unrealized, surprisingly unanticipated, yearning
with the comfort of basic human kindness and intimacy.
Soothing as chicken broth on a throat afflicted and inflamed,
a suffusion of nutrients with healing properties
instantly easing the scratchy irritation and raging hurt,
restoring my voice, however transient,
a reminder that discomfort and ailment are temporary.

It captivates me like the flickering flames in a fireplace
entrancing, dancing in colors, heat and light,
sinuous as the mathematical measures
of sound and rhyme that coalesce
in elevation to an unparalleled abstraction.
Creating movement internal, individual and intangible,
transcendent of worldly concerns and idioms
an impromptu transportation to destinations imprinted,
reveling in the wealth of sensation released
until I am gently settled back on bouncing feet.

Music of the Family Farm

Sizzling of fresh bacon
crack of eggs as they hit the pan
percolating coffee scenting the air
while biscuits rise and bake
before the rooster greets the sun.
Sleepy good mornings muttered
before heads bow, hands are folded
in reverent thanksgiving.
The clatter of cutlery on plates
dishes passed from hand to hand
with thank you echoing all around.

The radio blasting country music,
mooing, neighing, clucking,
snorting, snuffling, barking, meowing,
as stalls are mucked and hay is thrown,
eggs are gathered and water is drawn,
gardens are tended and produce gathered,
laundry is washed and hung to dry,
preserves are canned and stored away,
animals are tended to and fed,
Engines roaring or idling
As ground is cultivated
and crops are sowed, weeded, sprayed, mown,
gathered, harvested or stored.

Gospel strains and soars
as a community joins in praise
and joy on a bright Sunday morn.
Secretly whispered prayers for sunshine,
for rain, for strength, for enough.
Voices raised in chatter and laughter
as chores are done, playtime begun
and a feast is graciously prepared
under the loving care of Grand-mere,
Mama, and her bustling sisters.
Children's stomping feet through the halls
running down the stairs before
"Come" can be followed by "and Get it"

all rushing to be first at the table.
Chairs scrape across hardwood floors
Seats are settled and squabbles cease
heads bowed once again in prayer.

The soft distinctive pull on the pipe,
cherry scented smoke in circles overhead
alongside the easy creak of the rocking chair,
the porch swing and gently dragging feet
across faded white paint on slats underneath.
A hush falls as the sun sets over the horizon
like a crystal encrusted velvet curtain
dropping on a Shakespearian tragedy
and the moon takes center stage.
The symphony of crickets chirping
a sweet breeze kissing skin
while blowing mosquitos off target.
The dogs' exhausted sprawl,
dream chases and wuffling snores
inspire giggles to break the caesura.

A chorus of protesting wails remonstrate
the proclamation of bath and bed,
but shuffling feet follow sleepy nods
knowing the dawn comes early
for the ostinato rhythm on a farm.
Livestock and crops need tending
chores are unending.

Photo provided by Maria Braker

Music of a Thunderstorm

Lightning and the horizon
dancing the jitterbug
in the distance, not so distant.
See the flash, hear the crash
moving, flying oh so fast…
Feel the sizzle and the rumble
as it all settles into a syncopated
stroboscopic panorama
with the banshee song of the wind,
the discordant beating of the hail,
the rushing, roaring slide of the rain,
as the light show escalates
swiftly moving over the landscape
energy ramping into crescendo
as the thunder batters eardrums
and the lightning assaults the eyes…
Then the diminuendo
as the storm blows over
the horizon becomes a wallflower
as the lightning finds another partner,
rhythm returns with wind instruments
and the slow notes of a love song.

Music of An Old Country Church

Feet on well-worn wooden steps.
Good morning greetings echoed
with every creak of the entry.
Doffing of hats and skirts whispering,
faces glowing in their Sunday attire
and mostly on their best behavior.
Still, little boys giggle at exclamations
and duck little girls' retribution
after pulling braids and pigtails.
One glance from Mom curtails
shenanigans, separates hooligans,
and directs shuffling feet to take seats.
The Preacher begins the worship
raising his voice in a sermon.
Joyful noise echoes to the steeple
in psalms and the gospel,
spilling out into the brilliant morning
some whispering, some shouting
some sweetly mimicking angels
others tone deaf, off key
and blissfully unaware.
The Preacher's words rise and fall
weaving through it all
in reverence uplifting the congregation
transporting them to heaven
and bringing them gently back on a hymn.
Laughter, love and fellowship
follow as a mid-day meal is prepared
offered, served and shared
in the ultimate display of community
before returning to hearth and home.

Garden Chapel. Big Cedar Lodge.
Photo taken by Randy Thomas.

Music of a Strode Family Gathering

Doors opening and slamming
greetings with back pounding hugs
feet trooping through the house.
Spoons stirring and pan lids rattling
laughter, great booming laughter,
with Grandma's distinctive laugh
rising above the rest.
Football, basketball, or other sport
commandeering all televisions
triumphant roars following scores.
Rock and roll emanating
through the closed door to the basement
or from speakers around the pool
accompanied by GERONIMO
big splashes and screams.
Giggles, cackles and the sound
of running feet
followed quickly by shouts
of NO RUNNING IN THE HOUSE!!
Yells, screams, shouts, and more laughter
from the game of tag football
held in the open field across the street.
Heated words when it was deemed
visitors were too rough
or handsy with the GIRL.
A shrill whistle heard for literally miles
calls everyone in to eat.
The rattle of silverware against plates
ice hitting the bottom of glasses
effervescent drinks being poured
all overshadowed by conversations
sounds of appreciation, teasing,
good hearted tormenting and humor,
chairs scraping on hardwood
as seats are taken.
Then the room echoes in silence
as all heads are bowed, eyes are closed
and one voice is raised in prayer.

Thanks are given for the bounty
the opportunity to gather
for family and friends present or absent
blessings requested for the hands
that prepared the nourishment for our bodies
all in Jesus' name and the quiet chorus of Amen.
Once again the overwhelming, raucous music
of a large happy family resumes
and continues until the echoes of partings
wishes for safe travels and
promises to see each other again soon.

Whimsy and Imagination

Wielding the Hammer

Inspiration strikes
like hammer to anvil
molding the blank
to become a bright
sharp edged blade;
then melts away
like the smoke
of the quenching oil.

Alice Knows…

Inside the looking glass, Alice knows,
image lurks and mystery glows.
Illusion ------ or naught?
Senses doubting every thought
when solid as stone melts away,
romance and evil dance and play,
dragon's breath dews ice,
beside Merlin's magic faerie lights.
Classic tales soar and cry
while exploring the literary mind's eye.
Creating fantasy adventure
lasting more than a century
but passing a lifetime in a blink.
Myth and mystery weaving concentrically
silken threads confining truth unwise
for the true explorer to recognize.
        Inside the looking glass,
                Alice knows…
                        image lurks and
                                mystery glows.

Note: A reference to Lewis Carroll, "Alice in Wonderland"

Down the Rabbit Hole

Crystal ball, oh crystal ball,
Alice knows the way
into a realm of fantasy and dismay
where confusion rules and cards fall
in piles of immobile disarray
only disturbed from where they lay
by the rabbit's self-indulgent call...
 I'm late.... I'm late....
  for a very important date.

Crystal ball, oh crystal ball,
what would you display,
if into the past I could embark
on a mission to replay?
How different would the story align,
what fractures could be relieved?
What changes on the time line
would we see appear?
A nudge here and a shove there
to affect decisions made.
A well-placed smack to expel
fragments distorting the way.
Reflections in the mirror
redesigned, examined and assayed.
Significant events becoming clear
highlighting choices arraigned.
Where, now, would I be,
who would be by my side?
Would I be the same me
or someone unrecognized?
Would I love the same people,
lead an enhanced life,
or find greater happiness
wielding the surgeon's knife?

Was I meant to do more,
have a greater impact,
blast my way through closed doors,
drive myself to the apex?
Insecurity is a weakness
reviewing life in hind-sight.
Self-doubt will make you weep
and regrets dissatisfied.

Crystal ball, oh crystal ball,
I have no need of thee.
For wherever my chosen way leads
I'm content to follow the clarion's call
letting Alice take responsibility
for coaxing me under the tree.
The Mad Hatter's cackle follows our fall,
   Twinkle, twinkle little bat……
      How I wonder where you're at.

Note: A reference to Lewis Carroll, "Alice in Wonderland"

My Pensieve

My pen is my wand
floating as a feather wanders.
Drawing memories from my thoughts
flowing like gossamer images
scratched across the page.
Safely hidden away,
stored for another day
that they might be examined
with a new perspective,
seen through new eyes,
reviewed in a different light
where they cause no pain or harm.
Cleansed from the heart
and purged from the soul
like infection from a festering wound
halting self-flagellation
so healing can begin.

Note: A reference to J.K. Rowling, "Harry Potter and the Goblet of Fire".

Literary Receipt

The words are always there
floating around beneath my hair
time and space are needed to hear
the musical rhythm to be snared.

Relaxing under a warm shower
during the monotony of a long drive
quiet hours before family rises
mindless motions of repetitive chores.

Now comes the really tricky part
arrange the words in meaningful order
to evoke thought, memory or picture
illumination infused for others.

Natural Selection

The web is spun
      the fat spider waits,
dinner will come along
      in some silly fly.

The black cat stalks
      the quiet underbrush,
dinner will come along
      in some silly mouse.

The wolf slinks through
      the tall green grassland,
dinner will come along
      in some silly rabbit.

His fangs are sheathed
      as his trap is set,
dinner will come along
      in some silly woman.

The Snake's Seduction

Have you danced with the Devil in the pale moonlight?
Do the hounds of hell trail you through the blackest night?
Do you dream only nightmares when you close your eyes?
Do you speak with a tongue that will flay only lies?
Do your eyes glow with Satan's unquenchable hate?
Does his sinister laughter cradle your fate?
Does your smile give testament to life's pain and fear?
These questions reveal answers to your soul, I hear.
Yes, you've danced this jig in silvery lunar light
and your eternity will be the dark endless night.

I have also bathed in his unholy delight
we were a devilishly wondrous sight
He hurled and twirled me round and round
and finally tossed me heavenward bound
As much as I hate to here admit
it was a night I shall never forget
for after he'd tossed me so very high
he took me to hell upon a lie.

Note: Inspired by the Joker played by Jack Nicholson in the Warner Bros./Tim Burton 1989 movie "Batman"

Spelling Poetry

Prime the sounds to be found
with a wave of the mental wand;
syllables conjured and bound
to spark the spell on its round.

Once the words are there
glowing and dancing on air
intense concentration snares
musical rhythm as it flares.

Earth, water, ether and flame
spirits summoned to instigate
a litany of literary fascination
smoking forth the vital array.

Tenacity flowing into rhyme
energy of life's blood to combine
words into phrases sublime
images invoked and aligned.

Ridiculous, humorous or serious
magician's purpose is revealed
as incantation unfettered flies free
to enrapture all unaware.

Yearning strands of sorcery splinter
bursting like fireworks to empyrean
beguiling with light and color myriad
glamour, emotion and inspiration.

Pandora

Isolated innocence corrupted
set up for failure by blissful ignorance.
She knows no evil
is untouched by deceit.
She knows only the sweetness of water
the warmth of fire
the caress of the breezes
and the solidity of the earth beneath her feet.
She knows no grief or fear
only love and benevolence in prayer
the glow of radiant joy
the curiosity of a child with a new toy.
She is the key to opening the lock
releasing the latch on the enticing box,
The key that will set loose all hell on earth
allowing evil the freedom to play with every heart.

Song of the Mermaid

Don't fall for me
I'm as fickle as the sea.
One minute loving waves
touch and caress with spray.
The next they torture,
crashing, leaving only to return.

Never love the mermaid,
for my eyes of deep jade
hold only cold possession.
I'll lead you to confession,
and your love taken down,
to the very depths you'll drown.

The albatross soars,
a good omen ignored,
the mariner instead watches me.

Storm of Dragons

A flight of dragons graces
the super-heated afternoon sky,
gleaming in prismatic shades
among piles of clouds brilliantly white.
From the youngest fledgling,
struggling to keep the arduous pace
with newly minted wings,
to the grand dame
as she snaps reprimands
at juveniles demonstrating
their love of flight in hijinks and antics,
rolls, dives and chasing games.
The patriarch follows, lazily pulling shadows.
His immensity turns the clouds charcoal
and thunder reverberates from the earth below
with each powerful wing stroke.
Static electricity is enticed to gather
like sparklers on the 4th of July,
streaming in glowing splatters,
flowing into bolts randomly splitting the sky
and an impromptu lightening display
heralds a freakish summer thunderstorm
that drenches all in its wake
through blazing refracted sunlight.

*Unknown artist, found on the Mill Road
Fairy Garden Facebook page.*

Dancing with Moonbeams

The evening serenade begins
with the song of the crickets and cicadas
joined by the fireflies flickering like Bics
at an outdoor REO Speedwagon gig,
swaying this way and that, flutter and skip.
Raindrops splash in accompaniment
with thunder a distant rumbling rhythm
and lightning adding a fireworks blitz.

Hushed anticipation falls as the sky clears
and the full moon makes its appearance
hanging solitary with prismatic radiance,
while clouds, dark and heavy, play peekaboo
caressed fleetingly by moonbeams
streaking joyously on their descent,
excited to illuminate nature's soiree,
assured of their welcome to center stage.

Flirting with shadows, irradiating the night
waiting for the fairies to alight and ignite
shaking their dust in absolute delight,
coyly amplifying the moonbeams' light
sinuously dancing along the glowing paths
to the leaves, flowers and blades of grass
dripping with sparkling crystal splatter
flinging rainbows like shards of glass.

Respite

I sat watching in awe
ensnared as witness by what I saw.
The Fairies legal review to decide
ownership of a dew drop diamond
gracefully hanging on a single silken thread
dangling and sparkling in a wondrous web
capturing the morning glow
tossing razor edged shards to and fro
between the spider
and the fly.
Whose labor built the trap?
Whose lunch will be wrapped?
Whose landing dripped the drop?
Whose silk caught the plop?
Whose struggles made it grow?
Whose life expectancy is low?

The Photographer

Most frequently fleeting moments
worthy of capture require recognition
an eye to identify
reflexes to focus
with exact timing and shutter
to be photo frozen
or they are lost only to memory.

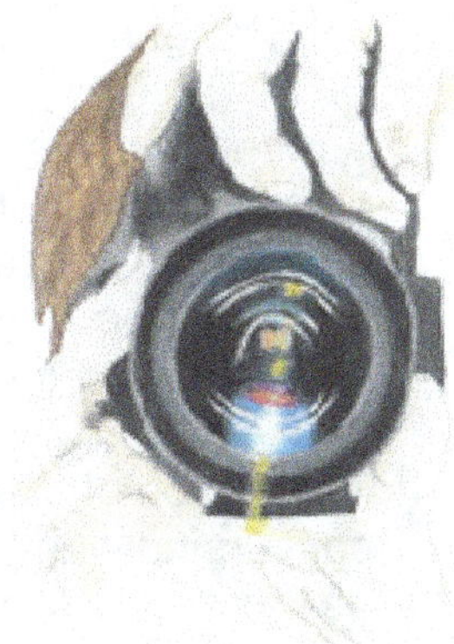

A Discussion of the Ages

Shakespeare, Yeats and Poe
sitting at a round table you know
discussing with Camelot as a whole
love lost, the subsequent woe,
and the darkness in a man's soul.

Arthur being not yet aware
of Lancelot and Guinevere's affair
waxes poetic on the beauty of amore
While his knights focus on their crusade
To find the Holy Grail.

Juliet's ghostly voice whispers
of Romeo's unfortunate lineage
foreshadowing the tragedy impending
the lovelorn couple as their families
proceed to intervene.

Yeats expounds upon the repetitious
death of cowards attempting to convince
that time and therefore history's
revolutions will continue
until the dancer meets the final ellipses.

A raven in all its dark splendor
alights quietly in the corridor
drawn by a rap rapping at the door
darkness there and nothing more
except for the thumping heard evermore.

The Prince of Denmark hovers
conversing with his skull about murder
as Mordred storms the castle's perimeter
ending this School of Night's deliberation
having devolved into atheism and insurrection.

The Masquerade

How could you know
behind the confident demeanor
is a scared shy little girl,
frightened of rejection,
looking to be loved for herself
not the façade she shows?

How could you know
her distractions are an escape,
social norms everyone enjoys
make her uncomfortable and edgy
like a misfit without vestiture,
more lonely than when she's alone?

How could you know
she would rather appear aloof than
reveal her shortcomings, true or imagined,
frightened to share thoughts and opinions
leaving herself open to ridicule
as the butt of the joke?

How could you know
self-doubt is her constant companion,
fear of a misstep holding her back,
too insecure in her abilities and facts
to openly share her perspicacity,
reticent, quiet, unassuming, invisible?

How could you know
when she wears a mask and cloak?

Photo taken by Jessica Rivera

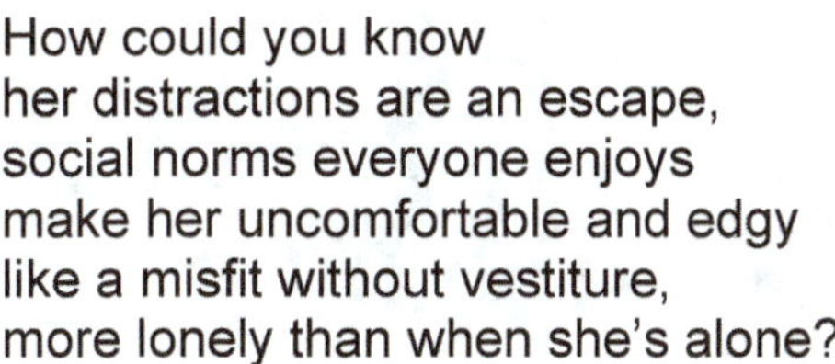

Chameleon

I find myself mimicking
blue that is wholly you
whether the deepest ocean
under Mother Nature's assault
or a summer sky cloudlessly clear

I find myself fading
under pink garishly present
overwhelmingly suppressive
pervasively negative

I find myself mimicking
green that is seen
in strivings of professionals
that surround me apathetically
during daily activities

I find myself fading
in charcoal of others' shadow
following with no vote
silenced in the cacophony

I find myself mimicking
yellows and reds that glow
radiantly from joyful souls
with purpose gathering
whether friends or family

I find myself fading
in the white backdrop of existence
easily could I blend and vanish
my absence going unnoticed

Façade

I live as one apart…
On the periphery.
An anachronism in my soul,
an oxymoron in my demeanor,
with periodic dissociative behavior.

No bubble or glass house,
but an invisible film
serendipitously surrounds me.
Tight as neoprene,
expansively flexible,
selectively permeable,
rigidly sealed to all
but wind and rain,
tears and pain.
Designed by environment,
molded by nurture.
A façade of enameled steel
while reality is fear,
self-doubt and insecurity.

I live as one apart…
dissociatively disrupted
but drawn to the laughter of others,
not knowing how to connect,
conform and be accepted for me.

Unconscious Focus

A single grain of sand in the palm of my hand.

Sometimes square
Sometimes hexagonal
Sometimes round

Round is the worst as
there are no edges to slow it down.
So hard on this single grain do I focus
that my hand seems to blow up and up and surround
like a balloon continually ascending.

Bigger and bigger
Rising with each breath
        Suffocatingly surreal and stifling

I'm on the outside in a box
as the balloon pervades the space
forcing me deeper and deeper into its excess
with no avenue of escape.
The pressure becomes intolerable.

On my chest
        On my head
                On my body

I wake drenched in sweat and screaming in distress.

Imperfect Seashells

The bits and pieces nobody wants
lying loosely in the sand
washed up as chips and fragments
cast off and lashed toward land.

Tourists prefer their seashells intact
scorning nature's imperfections
unmindful of beauty's illusion
splashed on the imagination.

Only those whose view is unimpaired
by ephemeral ideals of symmetry
will recognize and be ensnared
on the fractures, fissures and imagery.

These slivers and shards once whole
now discarded by the sea
could be souvenirs of a soul
awaiting conception and artistry.

Bluebird

You're reading a book
    A conversation starts
Your attention is pulled from the book
But your thoughts are still on what you read
    What a pretty picture on the wall
Movement on the TV from the corner of your eye
    Did you hear me??
Um yeah…
    Well?
Conversation continues
    A bird sings outside the window
    What a pretty song
    The radio is heard from a passing car
    A leaf is moved across the yard by the wind
    A cat jumps in your lap
You stroke his back and are caught by purring
Hello!! Are you listening??
Yes, I'm listening…
    Again the TV flashes something new
    A squirrel runs up a tree outside the window
    And jumps to another and then another tree
Your book calls you back
    Did you hear what I said??
I'm sorry… What?
Could you say that again?

Dinner Out

I glance around the restaurant
Dean and Frank for musical ambiance
accompanied by clinking
of dishes and silverware
young laughter from over there
and conversation everywhere.
We came early to beat the crowd
so who thought it would be this loud.
The next observation
slices like a sharp knife through the din,
assails and pierces the ears.
An elderly couple shoots glares
at a child's mother
as a he screams his displeasure,
obviously of the generation
where children are seen and not heard.
Further, the mother bears the brunt
because she is responsible for the runt
even though his father is across the table.
The waitress appears at my elbow
to jot down our inclination
with eyes only for my companion.
I must be invisible,
at the very least uninteresting.
My laughter joins the cacophony
as my husband's eyes are only for me,
and with a smirk at her I divulge
that the ticket and tip are mine.
Next a conversation between two twits
suffering from overinflated egocentrism
mocking the attention of a young father
who likely was just being hospitable.
Another child's ear splitting shrieks
slice through the air behind me.
At least this deafening noise
has an overtone of laughter and joy…
I guess I should have agreed
to that lovely glass of vino,
it was after all my favorite Moscato.
Instead of a glass, maybe the whole bottle…?

Historian's Creed

One man's truth is to another
fabrication and delusion.
Facts are colored by interpretation
viewed through the aperture
of culture, values and environment
without objectivity or detachment.
A true historian must mine through
the tailings of emotion and fanaticism
without vested interest in acceptance
of the resulting compendium chronicled,
while refusing to compromise integrity
under pressure of politics and propaganda.
The perception of black and white
is arbitrary and capricious
If discordant visit a local paint store
where white is Snow Day, Swiss Coffee
and Chantilly Lace
while black is Onyx, Salamander, Inkwell
and Cheating Heart
There is nothing simple about black and white
when gleaning the three sides of every truth.

In the Clouds

On the way home I saw...
King Arthur kneeling, head
bowed before Excalibur
encased in stone, watched
by the fae Sidhe sneaking
around on a nearby grassy knoll.

Zeus pulling down lightening
from tormented heavens. Pegasus
breaking free of Calibos' binding
chains. The leather armor encased
fist of Thorin raised in triumph
at the gates of his ancestral
mountain home. Guenhwyvar
materializing from ebony
at the call of her drow.

Blinding white stalagmites
reaching for the sky among clouds
stretched as thin and wispy
as cotton candy at the State Fair.

A dragon breathing pearly vaporous
fire across azure aether, her freshly
hatched offspring screaming
for their first meal. The volcano
over Pompeii spewing ash
hours before eruption. A phoenix
fully engulfed in fiery flame.

Neptune swimming across the sky,
trident in hand. Mermaids surfing
the crests of high tide. Dolphins
frolicking in frothy waves following
a ship with sails bellowing, the captain's
hook pointing the way. Peter Pan
propelled joyously by magic.

Red Riding Hood's grandmother,
in nightcap, facing down the wolf.
Geppetto sporting a pompadour fading
into the Man in the Moon. Briar Bear
resting between honey escapades.

The little Coppertone girl grasping
for a bright butterfly, dragging her teddy
with a floppy eared puppy trailing.

The bright swirling of God's light
on Mount Sinai. An angel swooping
to save a soul in free fall, wings
widespread and wondrously glowing.

Is it any wonder that I walk constantly
with my head in the clouds?

Old Man Bridge

Old Man Bridge spanning the Gasconade
built of wood beams and metal trusses
erected when the Model-T was an adolescent
and the Mother Road was in its infancy
winding carelessly through rocky hills,
thick forests and pockets of farmland
sporting cattle, horses, and any manner
of wonderful wildlife species

Old Man Bridge spanning the Gasconade
steadfastly supporting transit, heavy
commerce and tourist traffic
enduring the clip clop of horses' hooves
the rattle and roll of wagon wheels
the thump thump thump of rubber tires
with ever increasing groans and sways
evidence of the impact of time and weather

Old Man Bridge spanning the Gasconade
what fantastic sun rises you have greeted
watching over fisherman, boaters and floaters
swimmers, hunters and ever moving prey
What marvelous moonscapes you have created
as the beams reflect off the sparkling waters
and leaves rustle on the surrounding trees
over casting your manmade silhouette

Old Man Bridge spanning the Gasconade
how many of Mother Nature's tantrums
have you witnessed throughout the years
from tornados, lightening, thunder and floods
that rise to blanket you in water, debris and mud
to blizzards, layers of ice and wind enough
that trees crack and drop under the weight
scattered throughout the magnificent landscape

Old Man Bridge spanning the Gasconade
how did it feel to be sidelined and relegated
to a lonely frontage road traversed by residents
and fanatics in love with Old Route 66
replaced by a new sleek concrete interstate
with wider lanes separated east and west bound
asphalt instead of wood and no Parker, Pratt
and Warren Pony trusses to delight the eyes.

*This is a tribute to the old bridge spanning the Gasconade River south
of I-44 and east of Lebanon, MO, on historic Old Route 66. It was
constructed between 1922 and 1924 as part of the construction of the
Mother Road. It was closed December of 2014 due to safety issues.
Efforts to convince the State of Missouri to repair the bridge rather than
replacing it failed and a new bridge was constructed, but the old bridge
is still in place. Photo taken by Steve Miller*

Witches Castle

I can feel the proximity of the full moon
its pull both struggle and boon.
I trust I will be fully ensorcelled and ensconced.
The safety of all I love ensured by my beloved, Conna,
as she has since the beginning of my affliction.
No one is more blessed than I in matrimonial affection.

These words I found flourished across parchment,
bound in a journal buried with other regalia
yellowed with age, ink faded and so fragile,
written by the last Lord of the Witches Castle.

One night on the bluest of full moons,
one who thought he knew, but alas, misunderstood,
did unleash the beast on the unsuspecting
by unlocking a door on those purposely sequestered
fouling a spell laid best to enlist the deepest blessed sleep,
rendering a monster unconscious and harmless as the sheep.

I continued to decipher, struggling with strange words
scripted in long, flowing, nearly indecipherable scribble
spanning the page, frequently becoming lost and obscured,
arduously revealing a personal account of history.

Screams upon growls could be heard beyond the bailey
as blood did flow and gore did fly around those who tried to flee.
Targets they became whither they ran or were frozen in terror.
All fell to overwhelming rage, boundless and untethered,
released upon willing participants of unspeakable actions
perpetrated on those charged in Salzburg with witchcraft.

My eyes filled with blinding tears as I watched the scene
unfold across my mind like a horror film on a movie projector,
fleshing out whispered warnings and validating wards against evil
retold and believed by generation after generation.

*Teeth did elongate and snap, bones cracked and realigned
as hair sprouted from snout to tail, newly materialized.
Wolf-like but rising on two legs in semi-human stature,
my true nature enshrouded by this despicable creature.
Cursed to live, tortured by knowledge of what I have become
and the intolerable guilt of things I have done.*

A wolf howls in the forming twilight outside
terror grips my soul as I ponder the preternatural,
shadows surround me and goose bumps arise.
Is there truth in tales told to frighten visitors?

*This poem was inspired by an episode of Ghost Hunters. Photo was
obtained from a travel website.*

*The Moosham Castle, also known as Schloss Moosham or the Witches
Castle, is located In Austria. The castle was built in 1191 and was the
site of witch trials in the 1600s and werewolf hunts in the 1800s. It is
considered to be haunted. It is open to the public and contains a museum.*

Tessa

In an alternate reality I have a niece
with long blonde curls glowing
like an ornate halo,
bouncing in the slightest breeze.
Bright, sparkling, sky blue eyes
in a cherubic face. Milky pale skin
freckled and flushed pink
like that on a cherished china doll.
I visited her once. And awoke with my
heart overflowing with love.
She wore a dress in cornflower blue,
ruffled with lace. A strand of pearls
adorned her perfectly long
slender neck, matching drops at her ears.
She twirled for me in the caressing sunlight,
secure in her place in our hearts.
Gentleness radiated from her soul,
strength of character obvious,
with intelligence and wicked wit.
In an alternate reality I have a niece
with long blond curls and bright blue eyes.
Her name is Tessa.
Maybe I will be allowed to visit again…

Misty Adventure

My favorite color is the sky
in all of its many emotions.
To be a cloud
would be an adventure!!
I could take any shape…
cumulous to stratus,
opaque to nebulous.

Display the emotions in colors…
snowy white to the darkest black,
purple to fushsia, pink, and coral
reflecting the sun rising or setting;
blue, blue and more wonderful blue.

Display the emotions in storms, or not…
gray to black shattered by electricity,
the green before the freight train,
the brightest sparkling blue skies
interrupted by fluffy white clouds…

I could be Puff the Magic Dragon
on a flying carpet
under the watchful eyes of the Sphinx,
a crocodile carrying a frog
on a log raft under raised sail,
an eagle soaring high
wings majestically extended,
a lion and his lioness
stalking prey from concealment.
Clouds whipped around by a wicked wind,
or shooed gently by a kiss
blown from Mother Nature's lips.

My favorite color is the sky
in all of its many emotions.

Obituary of the Misunderstood Man

Herein depicts the legacy of the surly old man
who lived in the dilapidated house
passed the intersection of Alienated Circle
at the dead end of Judgement Way
who rejected pity and considered concern
the tool of nosy bodies and gossipy old hens.
The scary mean old man who preferred solitude
was suspicious of offered kindness
responded to greetings and pranks alike
with acerbic comments and nasty attitude
whose passing today went unremarked.
He is survived:

by a wooden leg
earned in armed combat
when he answered with alacrity
the call to serve his country
to defend liberty and freedom
to protect the weak
and liberate those wronged;

by a pocket watch from his namesake
who was killed by the railroad
as it grew this great nation
opening to a photo of his beloved
taken before grief put shadows in her hazel eyes
next to a youthful photo of his grandmother;

by the swinging gate at the front
of the dustbowl yard which cants
at an odd angle because his hands,
broken by a life of hard labor,
could no longer hold the tools to fix it;

by the empty house which long ago
forgot the echoing sound of feet running
on buffed and gleaming hardwood
between the giggles and laughter
of happy and healthy hearts;

by an empty wheelchair topsy-turvy in the dust
next to steps once used by visitors
warmly welcomed with open arms
to hearth and hospitality
always ready with sweet and savory
never refused or begrudged respite;

by an empty porch swing
tethered precariously by one chain
shifting in the wind chains clanging
like Jacob Marley's as he warned
Ebenezer of impending doom
instead of the quiet creaking heard
from a gentle sway while two hearts
watched a stunning sunset and held hands;

by the discordant piano in the front room,
once lovingly treasured and polished
now buried in dust and swollen with moisture,
on which his beloved played God's gospel
and taught many a youngster her love of music.
Not a key has resonated nor a note sounded
since the day his world imploded
and she was called home to Jesus;

by a stack of tearstained letters,
bundled together in a red ribbon,
written home during that long ago war
documenting love and longing
with a few daily details, but none of the horror,
now only stories in history books
but which haunted his dreams until today;

by battered medals on faded ribbons
in a plain worn wooden box
of which he never spoke and felt undeserving,
touchstones reverently worn smooth
through years of tears after wracking nightmares
full of horror, bloodshed and loss;

by beautifully carved crosses
within a weather beaten
white paint peeling picket fence

out back under the willow tree.
The smallest ones marking their little lambs
each with a name and set of dates
the longest spanning only a handful of years
the shortest but a few weeks;

by the rusty tractor sitting in the barn
whose engine won't turn over
on tires flat from dry rot
the nests of birds and rodents protruding
from darkened openings;

by the empty stalls where beloved horses
used to whinny greetings and stamp
their impatience for his attention
prancing when saddles and brushes appeared
or nuzzling in affection with fuzzy soft noses
nibbling on hats and hair as stalls were mucked,
water and feed were refreshed;

by the garden once beautifully arranged
rows straight and perfectly tended
yielding a rainbow of color
on plants raised for ease of harvest and beauty
produce canned and stored for winter's repast
flowers cut and arranged for sight and scent
now overgrown with thistle and crabgrass
blackberry vines unchecked and useless;

by the acres and acres behind the barn
that used to support sweetcorn and beans
cattle, hogs and free range chickens
now empty, bare and lifeless;

by the apathy of repossession and demolition
dozers poised ready to dance to the jig
prescribed by the bank
as the way is opened for progress
and this postage stamp rendering
falls to the unstoppable movement
of corporate ownership.

Pain Killers

Ace rides in on a fast horse,
his cowboy armor glinting in the sunlight,
tips his hat to the damsel in distress
then dismounts to challenge
the black hat wearing thugs
stirring everything up and causing pain.
Meanwhile his friend Ice hangs outside
the enflamed battle zone
pushing back the heated crowd
forcing paths of entry to constrict,
easing the irritated Nervous Nellies
and smoothing the inflammation
into a state of calm and pain relief.

Exploration of Black

What thoughts are engendered by black?

Beauty
The glinting, glowing feathers of a Raven's wing,
light glancing off black filled with blues and greens.
The waterfall of Native American hair glistening
as it sways gracefully in ancient dance and ritual.
Pinpoints of pure white sparkling against midnight
through darkness over the ocean, no land in sight,
as constellations guide a sailor home.
The eerie aloneness of the wildest territory known,
surrounded by an endlessly darkened sky
stargazers watching a shooting star by moonlight.

Imagination
Spooky trees swaying, leaves rustling in the wind.
Dracula's billowing cape lined in crimson.
The silhouette of a cat arched and hissing.
The wart, hat, kettle and broomstick signature.
Haunted shadows circulating the house on tiptoes.
Werewolves, backlit by the full moon, howling.
Temperature plummets, breath becomes evident
as local ghosts float and wickedly flit.

Sophistication
The epitome of style and elegance,
flowing ballroom grandeur of formal events.
The perfect stunning, demure little dress
with stiletto heels and silk encased legs,
flashy rocks spiking sparkles everywhere,
escorted by top hat and tailed Emperor penguins
with glaring mirror finished, tapping, patent leather,
cufflinks, boutonniere, oozing high fashion and wealth.

Adventure
Asphalt seen before dawn or after gloaming
eaten by the hungry tires on my time machine
during the escape from an endless journey,
racing into the mystery of what tomorrow brings,
joy, love, growth, satisfaction, loss, grief
confusion, insight, evolution… discovery.

Pain
Pervading the Stygian depths of sorrow
where light refuses to illuminate a mourner's soul,
slowly being crushed under overwhelming loss.
Desolation drowns the soul's windows
and angels' tears prove incapable of cleansing
or enlightening the darkness.
So they drench graveside whisperers,
further infusing misery into a ceremony,
orchestrated by a man in cassock and collar,
intended to provide sacrament and comfort
for those steeped in doubt and torment.

Fear
Close your eyes and be fascinated
by the shifting shapes of moving shadows
drifting and swirling in rhythm with circulation.
Darkness dense as the deepest subterranean position
where you cannot see the hand before your visage
accompanied by echoing sound amplification.
Staring into an abyss fighting the dizziness
that comes as twin to ambiguity,
or submerged in depths of watery suffocation
unbearably cold where light cannot insinuate.

Evil
The pirate flag whipped wickedly on the horizon.
Shrouding cowards burning a cross in persecution.
Little Boy and Fat Man dropped to stop a world war.
Saran gas released into a subway horror.
Concentration camps for ideology or ethnicity.
Powdered poison in envelopes striking terror.
Smoke, dust, and fire deafening Oklahoma City.
Al-Qaida flags flying over Fallujah in 2014.
ISIS kidnapping and beheading innocents.

Enlightenment
The pervasive absence of illumination
perpetuated by unbridled ignorance
rectified by opening minds with information.
The introduction of curiosity and literacy
learning to question and investigate
inspiring the light of lucidity
eliciting an explosion of imagination
followed by freedom in the color ambit.

I Dreamed in Rainbows.

There was a time I dreamed in rainbows

When life was music and light,
dancing among clouds of butterflies,
sweet breezes on a Spring night,
the scent of roses and firefly flight.

There was a time I dreamed in rainbows

When life was bursting with glee
despite those who misunderstood me.
Hidden behind a quiet demeanor
my truth in kaleidoscope glimpses revealed

There was a time I dreamed in rainbows

When life was limited only by imagination,
full of opportunity and self-expression,
interpretive art in fluid motion,
before I realized the darkness of deception.

There was a time I dreamed in rainbows

The fallacy of rose-colored glasses
swept the landscape monochromatic
and all that was pixie dust magical
was stripped away by harsh reality.

There was a time I dreamed in rainbows

Martha Maggie Miller was welcomed into the world on a beautiful Spring evening in Springfield, Illinois. Her Father barely survived her birth because he was late, and she was early. At least that's how her Mother told the story... She is an Environmental Professional and works for the Army after retiring from military service. She has a Bachelor of Arts degree with primary studies in Biology and English Literature. Yeah, she was often the recipient of incredulity and inquiry regarding her choice of studies. Heartfelt Snippets is a poetry manuscript containing snippets and snapshots, showcasing significant moments, both serious and humorous, with insights into her thoughts and emotions. Several of her poems were published while she was in college in their literary magazine. She has participated in poetry contests with some success, but this is her first published book. She hopes it brings laughter, inspires thought, tugs on your heartstrings, and most importantly strikes a chord of understanding and connection.